Infinite Selling

The modern approach to high-velocity
revenue generation and realization

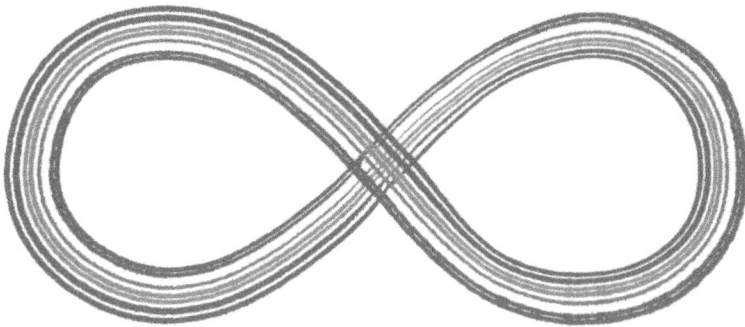

James A. Barton and Matt Webb

First published in Great Britain by Practical Inspiration Publishing, 2026

ISBN   9781788609265 (paperback)
       9781788609258 (hardback)
       9781788609272 (ebook)

EU GPSR representative: LOGOS EUROPE, 9 rue Nicolas Poussin, LA ROCHELLE 17000, France Contact@logoseurope.eu

Want to bulk-buy copies of this book for your team and colleagues? We can customize the content and co-brand *Infinite Selling* to suit your business's needs.

Please email info@practicalinspiration.com for more details.

Practical Inspiration
Publishing

This book is dedicated to everyone who has helped Matt and me with our careers to date, from our exceptional clients who have trusted us with their seller and leaders, to those who have supported, guided, mentored, and believed in us.

More importantly, this book is dedicated to the amazing team at Mentor Holdings and Mentor Group; we would never have even been here without them. It's our honour to work with you; thank you to each and every one of you.

Lastly, this book is dedicated to the art and profession of selling, and all of you who partake of this noble craft. Selling truly makes the world go round, so be proud of who you are and let's make our buyers even prouder.

Contents

Part 3: Infinite results, endless flow

Foreword by Peter Cowgill

When Matt and James approached me about writing this foreword, I was immediately intrigued by their vision for *Infinite Selling*. Throughout my nearly two decades at the helm of JD Sports, I witnessed firsthand how dramatically the retail and sales landscape can transform – and how critical it is to stay ahead of these changes rather than merely respond to them.

As someone who helped guide JD Sports from a high street retailer to a global powerhouse with a £355.2 million headline profit, I've always understood that success hinges on two fundamental principles: valuing the consumer; and embracing innovation. These principles are at the heart of what Matt and James explore in these pages.

The modern sales environment demands a different approach from the playbooks of yesteryear. During my time expanding JD internationally and building our online presence, I learned that staying 'in tune with millennials and Generation Z' wasn't just helpful, it was essential. Today's successful sales professionals must similarly tune in to changing customer expectations and the transformative technologies reshaping how we connect with and serve our markets.

What particularly resonates with me about *Infinite Selling* is its practical approach to artificial intelligence (AI). In my experience across retail and, more recently, with ventures such as Applied Nutrition, I have observed how businesses that intelligently adopt new technologies consistently outperform those that cling to outdated methods. Matt and James do not merely theorize about AI in sales, they provide a roadmap for implementing it in ways that genuinely drive results.

Having built and led teams through significant market evolutions, I appreciate the book's focus on the human element of selling. Even as we embrace AI and other technologies, understanding people – their motivations, preferences, and behaviours – remains the cornerstone of effective selling. This book brilliantly balances technological innovation with the fundamentally human aspects of the sales process.

For sales leaders navigating today's complex business environment, *Infinite Selling* offers invaluable insights into creating what I've always viewed as essential: a growth mindset throughout your organization. The strategies outlined here will help you not merely adapt to change but harness it as a competitive advantage.

In my current chapter as Chairman of The Fragrance Shop and as an investor in Applied Nutrition, I continue to see how the principles Matt and James outline – particularly around leveraging data and technology to enhance human decision-making – create tangible business value. Their approach isn't theoretical; it's battle-tested and practical.

Whether you're a seasoned sales director or just beginning your career, the techniques and perspectives in this book will equip you to sell more effectively in a world where AI is rapidly becoming not just an advantage but a necessity. Matt and James have created something special here – a forward-looking yet grounded guide to selling in the age of artificial intelligence.

I'm confident *Infinite Selling* will become an essential resource for anyone serious about sales excellence in the modern era.

Peter Cowgill

Introduction:
Sales is dead; selling is alive

The world of selling has undergone seismic shifts since we first began shaping these ideas in 2015. At that time, while working to reinvent the sales process for a global technology leader, we could already sense the ground shifting beneath our feet.

The traditional paradigms were beginning to fragment, and the expectations of both buyers and sellers were evolving rapidly. Yet, as is often the case, the demands of execution took precedence, and the deeper work of reimagining sales was put aside.

By 2019, the imperative to rethink selling had resurfaced, but we found ourselves questioning the need for yet another sales book. The market was saturated, and if we are honest, imposter syndrome crept in, stalling our momentum. We explore these internal saboteurs in more depth in Chapter 2, suffice to say they can be formidable barriers to progress.

Then the pandemic struck. While it was an extraordinarily challenging period, it also served as a catalyst for transformation in our profession. The overnight shift to remote work and virtual engagement forced both buyers and sellers to adapt, accelerating changes that might otherwise have taken years. The notion that sales could remain rooted in its old ways was quickly dispelled; digital channels became the norm, and the buyer's journey became more fragmented and self-directed than ever before.

However, the most profound disruption has emerged since 2023 with the rapid advancement and widespread adoption of artificial intelligence (AI). AI is no longer a peripheral tool; it has become central to the selling motion.

Today's buyers leverage AI-powered assistants to research, compare, and even shortlist solutions without ever engaging a human salesperson. For sales professionals, this means that the old model, where the seller controlled information and guided the process, has been fundamentally upended.

Yet, as AI automates the transactional and analytical aspects of selling, the uniquely human elements – empathy, creativity, emotional intelligence, and the ability to build trust – have become even more critical.

And this is where we believe Infinite Selling® (which has a registered trademark) can make a real difference, as the Infinite Loop can help to clarify how what we do in sales needs to be a constant and connected action rather than a series of separate actions.

If you, as we should, consider the buyer at the centre of everything we do, all our actions, whether human or AI-driven, should radiate from that.

In the diagram below, you can see that there is a motion before the buyer (Revenue Generation) and a motion after (Revenue Realization). Traditionally, each of these actions is a separate, even siloed, area or department, but it should be clear that for best success, they need to connect and work together and move, and in the words of author Stephen Covey, in his book *The 7 Habits of Highly Successful People* (Covey, 2004), move from independence to interdependence.

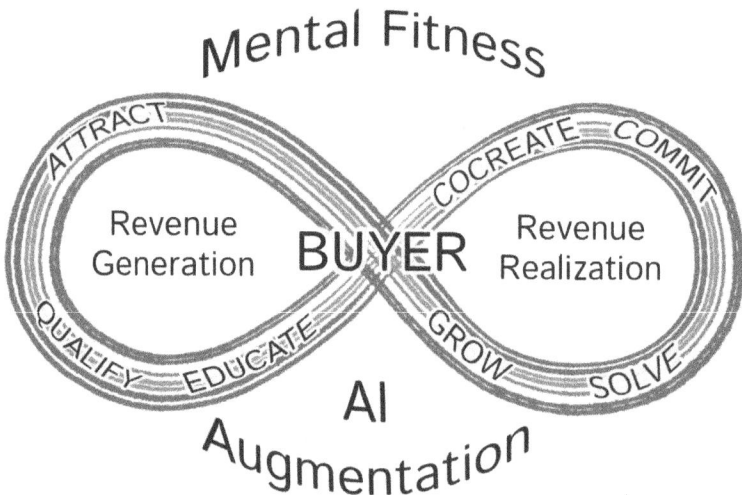

We will continue to explore this theme throughout the book, but you should view this as a central theme with the buyer always at the centre.

Sales is dead

I am going to say something that may be a bit weird for a book on selling, but it is something I believe at my very core: Sales is dead.

If this is true, this is going to be a short book! But let me explain. While sales is, in my opinion, dead, selling is very much alive and kicking! And, while it may seem a trivial and possibly even pedantic change in words, 'selling' best describes what is happening in today's market. For years, we have seen the concept of sales (a simplistic definition of sales is simply the exchange of money for goods or services), with hundreds, if not thousands, of books written on the topic, but with today's market changes, it is no longer viable as a standalone function.

Research from (Gartner, 2021) shows that customers spend only 17% of their buying journey interacting with a sales team. So, where are they spending their time?

I suggest the answer lies in the marketing department. They produce the content that the buyer consumes, which helps them decide to progress along the buying journey. And herein lies the major issue.

While some work has been done to integrate sales and marketing in recent years, it is still occurring in a non-collaborative manner. The rise of the CRO (Chief Revenue Officer) is helping, but even then, they generally manage two separate departments rather than one truly integrated function focused on revenue.

We will explore this more in Chapter 3, but until sales and marketing see themselves as one function, the function of selling, there will always be a major disconnect in our Infinite Loop, and the gap will only get bigger.

For us, there is only one metric that matters: revenue realization (you'll learn more about that in later chapters).

This, for us, is ultimately what we are doing: realizing revenue. It requires a wonderful and elegant dance between what we know as marketing, the sales teams, and customer success.

This is why we called this whole concept 'Infinite'. It is that constant motion between everyone, with a singular goal with the buyer in the centre. And it doesn't ever stop.

If it's done right, there is a perpetual relationship with our buyers as we continue to serve their needs, solve their problems, and help us all succeed.

Selling is a profession, not just a career

Another nail in the coffin for sales today is the growing change in how the next generation of workers wants to be seen.

Matt and I have often laughed at each other because, when asked what we do, we rarely mention the word 'sales'. This is because sales are often associated with the darker side of manipulation: being dishonest or disingenuous. For some, particularly those outside of sales, 'sales' is seen as a career for loud, obnoxious types who are gifted in speaking and driven by money. In fact, a common phrase is that sellers (as in people who work in sales) are coin-operated. If you want to see results, you must put the coin in the slot.

However, the profession of selling should not be viewed this way. When we consider the true heart of selling, we see that people do not get what they need unless something is bought and sold. Worse still, entire economies are measured by how much is traded. No sales equals no growth, which results in a reduction in the quality of our lives.

I know there is a debate between two factions of economists as to whether GDP (gross domestic product) is the right metric to measure economic growth, and I tend to agree that it's not. Even if you say happiness should be the measure, if you are unable to purchase the basics for survival, happiness is not going to be very high.

Selling is part of everyday life. It happens to us all, all the time, so to consider something so important as something dirty or a lower-class career is simply not giving it its due.

With *Infinite Selling*, we are looking to make a change. By bringing in concepts about authenticity, honesty, and even well-being, we want selling to be recognized as the lynchpin of our economies again – to bring back a golden age when being a seller is not something to be ashamed of.

This is not just an opinion that Matt and I share alone. If you look at the research on what the younger generation of sellers wants, they are no longer coin-operated.

Research from Deloitte (2023) shows that this generation values salary less than others. They are more interested in contributing to a fair, ethical, and good world.

Then take this further and consider not only sellers but also the next generation of buyers. They want to buy from companies and people that reflect and align with their own values.

This will require us to think again about what we teach our sellers. Are the generally aggressive and overly misogynistic terms commonly used in sales still appropriate?

Is it really about who has the power? Is it still just about won or lost sales? Are we still going to have boot camps? Are we still in the trenches? Do we still need battle cards?

Is it even truly a battle?

It really is time for change, and the benefits are clear. Not just for now but for the ongoing profession and the larger economy.

As revenue generators, we are responsible for a large amount of how the economy performs. If we aren't generating revenue, then we are not generating production. We are not creating jobs, and thus we are not creating taxes. A bit dramatic, I know, but this is just some of the power we hold, and we should be proud of it.

The importance of mental fitness

But there is a part that sellers don't talk about – something that a great many people struggle with and goes unspoken, partially because of the overtly masculine sales environment and partially because we are still not good at speaking and talking about it: our mental fitness.

This is such an important concept for us that we will dedicate an entire chapter to it. Rather than ignoring it or pretending it's not an issue, we want to tackle it head on and build it into the core of the INFINITE methodology.

We see strong mental fitness as foundational to our success. Without this strong foundation, everything you build on top is on very shaky ground, and it's not surprising that we see the shocking average tenures that we currently do, and the significant costs associated ((McKinsey & Company, 2021) believe this to be at least 5x the quota of the salesperson who left).

If we can look to build support to strengthen mental fitness as part of the process, it becomes part of the fabric of the business.

We will explore this further in Chapter 2, but look at some of the stats to whet your appetite:

- Poor mental health costs the global economy over US$1 trillion annually in lost productivity, with projections rising to US$6 trillion by 2030 (World Health Organization, 2024).
- UK employers face £51 billion in annual costs from poor mental health, mainly due to presenteeism and absenteeism, with nearly half of all productivity losses linked to mental health (Centre for Mental Health, 2024).
- Presenteeism, working while unwell, remains the most significant contributor to lost productivity, costing UK employers £41.8 billion a year (RoSPA, 2024).
- Investing in workplace mental health delivers a strong return, with every US$1 spent yielding US$4–6 in improved health and productivity (McKinsey Health Institute, 2025).

It's easy to see that a small investment here could yield significant benefits for the bottom line. This is also about being human. Recognizing that we all struggle with mental fitness from time to time and fostering an organization with a mentally healthy and fit team means it will be a more attractive and enjoyable workplace.

Whether this resonates with you or not, it is a reality we will all need to resolve.

Are methodologies still valid?

This book is not just about discussing sales topics; we aim to provide you with a brand-new methodology that is fit for purpose in a changing world. When I say brand-new, I mean 'net new'.

One of the challenges we have faced in the last ten years of building enablement solutions for our buyers is that the methodologies used were either outdated or modifications of a selling style that has been superseded.

In doing our research for this book and for our methodology, it was shocking just how old the existing sales methodologies were and how many of them were a modification of the original selling skills courses taught by Xerox in the 1970s. When we think of what has changed, the relevance of these seems to fall away. To be fair, there has been an effort to update these methodologies for the current day, but they are still based on outdated thinking and environments.

This is why we wanted to start again from scratch: to develop a methodology that was born in today's environment, meets the needs of today's buyers, and is actionable by the next generation of selling professionals.

So, yes, methodologies are still valid; they just need to change.

Ready to explore the infinite possibilities? Onwards!

Part 1

The foundations of Infinite Selling

Chapter 1

The Infinite seller: A guide, not a dictator

In our introduction, we highlighted the pressing need for change, especially in how we perceive sales and marketing. We'll explore this more in Chapter 3, but for now, let's consider these three pivotal statistics:

- By 2025, 80% of B2B (business-to-business) sales interactions between suppliers and buyers will occur in digital channels (Gartner, 2022).
- More than half of large B2B purchases (over US$1 million) will be processed through digital self-serve channels (Forrester, 2024).
- Some 19% of B2B decision-makers are already implementing generative AI use cases for buying and selling, with another 23% in the process of doing so (McKinsey & Company, 2025).

These figures should send a chill down the spine of anyone involved in developing enablement and transformation programmes. Similarly, sellers must contemplate what these changes entail, as traditional selling methods are being redefined. Adaptation is no longer optional; it is imperative for maintaining relevance.

Let's unpack each of these insights.

Digital channels: The new norm

Gartner's prediction that 80% of B2B sales interactions will be digital by 2025 underscores a significant shift in buyer behaviour (2025b). To grasp this, we must first understand what constitutes a digital channel and its inherent advantages.

Digital channels have surged in importance for both B2B and B2C (business-to-consumer) selling. They enable businesses to connect globally, transcending time zones and physical boundaries. Unlike traditional methods, digital channels prioritize providing buyers with the information they need to make informed decisions, often without real-time interactions.

This approach reduces costs associated with travel and other expenses, saving time and enhancing efficiency for both buyers and sellers – a true win-win.

Moreover, digital channels facilitate ongoing communication and engagement, fostering trust and loyalty. For instance, email marketing campaigns can inform clients about new offerings, while social media platforms allow for sharing valuable insights and engaging in meaningful conversations.

Another significant advantage is the wealth of data and analytics these channels provide. Tools can track website traffic, visitor behaviour, and conversion rates, offering actionable insights to optimize strategies and enhance user experiences.

In essence, digital channels empower buyers with information and provide sellers with broader reach, cost savings, and valuable intelligence.

Redefining the seller's role

With the rise of digital channels, the traditional seller's role is undergoing a transformation. The skills once perfected to guide buyers through stages, influence decisions, and add value are being challenged.

To reclaim their value in this new landscape, sellers must focus on two key areas.

- **Maximizing impact in direct interactions:** Even as digital channels dominate, there remains a crucial 20% of interactions where sellers can make a significant impact.

- **Integrating into the digital journey:** Understanding and influencing the 80% of the buyer's journey that occurs digitally.

We will explore these aspects further in this chapter, outlining the attributes required for success in this evolved selling environment.

The shift towards self-service

Forrester's insight that more than half of large purchases will be processed through digital self-serve channels highlights a growing preference for autonomy in the buying process.

This trend emphasizes the need for a digital-first approach, where content and value propositions are front and centre. Sellers must ensure that digital touchpoints are optimized to enable smooth transactions.

The integration of AI in sales

The integration of AI into the sales process is no longer a futuristic concept; it is a present reality. McKinsey reports that 19% of B2B decision-makers are already implementing generative AI use cases, with an additional 23% in the process.

AI's capabilities extend beyond automation; it offers predictive insights, enhances personalization, and streamlines processes. For instance, AI can analyse data to identify potential leads, forecast sales trends, and provide recommendations for engagement strategies.

Embracing the hybrid model

Gartner's research reveals that 75% of B2B buyers prefer a rep-free sales experience. This preference underscores the importance of a hybrid model that combines digital self-service with human interaction. Sellers must be prepared to engage when needed, offering expertise and support to complement the digital journey.

As you can see, selling is undergoing a profound transformation. Digital channels, self-service preferences, and AI integration are reshaping how buyers and sellers interact. To thrive in this environment, sellers must evolve, embracing technology, honing new skills, and adopting a strategic, customer-centric approach.

By aligning with these trends and adapting to the what's happening, not only can sellers remain relevant but also drive meaningful engagement and success in the modern marketplace.

So how different is this from where we currently are and what we are currently teaching our sellers?

The truth is, it's very different, as what we are teaching largely does not reflect the above reality. Today's sellers need different skills, and sellers need different attributes.

We must move away from lone wolves, hunters, farmers, challengers, etc. Selling has changed and moved on.

But sellers can still add huge value if focused in the right place.

The attributes of the Infinite seller

As mentioned earlier, what got us here will not take us there, and this applies equally to the makeup and qualities of successful sellers in the evolving selling environment. Of course, some core skills are still relevant, and I am not suggesting that we should abandon everything, but there is a noticeable shift in focus away from the skills we previously valued towards something more suited to today.

It's important to recognize that some good sellers will continue to use the old selling skills and achieve notable success, but the new attributes will set apart the good from the excellent.

So, what attributes are important for a highly successful seller, today?

In our research over the past decade, we have identified the following seven attributes that distinguish good sellers from excellent sellers.

These are sellers who (in no particular order) are:

- digitally literate
- buyer focused
- agile
- strategic thinkers
- continuous learners
- revenue-oriented, and
- values-driven.

Let's explore each one, but if you are interested in learning more about where you may fit in with these new attributes, you can take our free Infinite Seller Attributes test. Simply head to www.InfiniteSelling.com/Attributes and get an assessment and a free report on what you can do to move the needle (if needed!).

Being digitally literate

Being digitally literate is more than just knowing how to use a computer or browse the internet. Those are table stakes! It's about having the skills and knowledge to effectively educate your buyers and stakeholders about your products or services online. Being digitally literate is critical for any seller to succeed.

To be a digitally literate seller, you need to understand the various online platforms available to you. Whether it's social media, AI, or your own website, you need to know how to use these platforms to showcase your products and services. What's important here is not what you are comfortable with or what channels you use, but rather knowing and using the channels your buyers and their stakeholders use.

As the seller, we must be comfortable leading the way and demonstrating how new technologies, ideas, or concepts can benefit the buyer and our organizations. A digitally literate seller is comfortable taking the lead and not being stuck in their ways or simply following others.

As we have discussed before, the Infinite Loop focuses on revenue, which means a single function driven to create revenue. Therefore, rather than delegating content development to marketing, we must take responsibility for ourselves and support the team in creating engaging content that will capture your target audience's attention. We will explore this more in Chapter 5.

Another critical skill is the ability to analyse and interpret data. You might think, 'Oh great, more numbers to deal with', but hear me out: analysing and interpreting data is essential for any seller looking to grow their business and make informed decisions.

First off, data analysis allows you to track the performance of your products or services. You can see which items are selling well and which ones are not, allowing you to adjust accordingly as a team. You can also track buyer behaviour and preferences, allowing you to tailor your offerings to their needs better.

But it's not just about the numbers. Interpreting data allows you to make sense of what's going on in your business. You can identify patterns and trends, and use this information to develop strategies to help you stay ahead of the competition. You can track the quality of your pipeline and look at the trends to show you the best approaches and selling activities to help you and your buyer succeed. And with AI, this becomes even easier.

Health warning: *You need to understand AI as well as the data, as you must check its answers, given its tendency to wander off occasionally* (don't we all!).

When we consider that we are all part of the revenue function, all of the above is selling. You may view this as a problem for Revenue Ops or the marketing team, but it is not. It is an issue for us all to address now, working together. Sure, some individuals possess a more natural aptitude for numbers, but that doesn't mean we can ignore them.

Being digitally literate isn't just about your technical skills; it's also about connecting with your buyers on a personal level. This involves understanding their needs and preferences, and communicating with them effectively. You must be able to respond to buyer inquiries promptly and professionally, as well as utilize social media and other online platforms to engage with your buyers and foster relationships.

In short, being a digitally literate seller means having the ability to navigate the digital landscape with ease and confidence. It means having the technical skills, marketing knowledge, and customer service skills to succeed in the online marketplace.

If you want to be a successful seller in today's world, you need to make sure you're digitally literate. Trust me, your business will thank you for it!

Being buyer focused

Being buyer-focused means putting your buyers at the centre of everything you do. It means understanding their needs, preferences, and pain points – and using that information to shape your selling strategy.

It's about creating a buyer-centric culture that values feedback and fosters loyalty.

One of the key benefits of being buyer focused is that it enables you to create products and services that genuinely meet the needs of your target audience. By listening to your buyers and comprehending their pain points, you can develop solutions that address their problems and enhance their lives. This, in turn, can result in increased loyalty, retention rates, and repeat business.

It's also about providing excellent service – in other words, going above and beyond to ensure that your buyers are satisfied with their purchases and overall experience with you and your business. It means being responsive to their inquiries, providing clear and concise information, and being willing to make things right if something goes wrong.

This is part of the Infinite Loop, as the dance must move from finding opportunities to securing and developing the revenue we already have. The current trend to move to a customer success model is great (and long may it continue) and sellers need to support this function, not just palm it off. Blindly passing it on and considering it to be 'not our problem' is one of those behaviours that will not help us to achieve the right buyer experience.

Being buyer focused is also about creating a buyer-centric culture within your organization. This means instilling a mindset that puts the buyers first in everything you do. It means actively seeking out feedback and using that information to improve our offerings and how we present it.

As already mentioned regarding being digitally literate, we need to be comfortable and skilled in our communication across the modalities that our buyers are using. This buyer-centric approach will be critical when we discuss the concept of a buyer map in Chapter 5.

Being agile

As any gymnast will tell you, being agile is the ability to move quickly and easily, forming an essential part of the seller's makeup. The ability to adjust, change, and move at the same pace (or quicker) than our buyers is essential.

A buyer might change their mind, a competitor might come out with a new AI product or service, or a global pandemic might hit! As a seller, you must adapt to these changes quickly and faster than your competition.

Being able to pivot, when necessary, means changing your strategy instantly. It means thinking on your feet and creating creative solutions to problems. Let me give you an example.

Let's say you're a seller who specializes in selling data analysis software. Your biggest competitor just launched a new AI feature that blows your product out of the water. Suddenly, your buyers are asking for this feature too. Now, you have a choice. You can stick with your old product features and risk losing buyers to your competitor, or you can pivot and start to develop something similar or at least develop a strategy that allows you to position your product favourably, considering the new feature from your competitor.

If you are agile, you can pivot quickly and effectively. To achieve this, you must be comfortable with both change and ambiguity.

Change is difficult for many, but history is filled with organizations and individuals who believed they knew best, failed to adapt, and ultimately lost. Kodak, Blockbuster, and Blackberry, to name just a few, exemplify those who wished they had pivoted.

Change also often comes with ambiguity. A lack of clarity on the direction or next steps can be equally hard for people. Taking the example earlier, developing a comparative feature to the competitor might take weeks, months, or even years. Knowing how long it will take will be a mystery while the developers devise a plan.

All this is completely out of the seller's control. Therefore, we need to consider what we can do amidst the uncertainty. Those who are comfortable with the unknown and who can consider what they can do will be the most successful.

Don't get me wrong here. Having a plan is essential. But the key is to have a plan that's flexible, a plan that can be adjusted as needed, and a plan that allows for agility.

Think of it like a game of football (soccer, to be more specific, but you can adjust to make this fit your favourite sport).

You have a game plan going in. You know who your opponent is, their strengths and weaknesses, and how you will play. But once the game starts, things can change. Maybe your opponent switches up their strategy. Maybe your star player gets injured. Maybe the referee makes a bad call. As a team, you need to be able to adapt to these changes and adjust your strategy on the fly. That's agility.

Strategic thinker

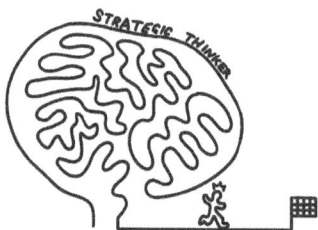

Building on being agile also requires the ability to be a strategic thinker – someone who can look at the bigger picture and devise a plan of action to achieve the goal. Just like a master chess player, you need to have a plan and execute that plan flawlessly. And that's where being a strategic thinker comes into play.

Being a strategic thinker involves examining the market, the competition, your own strengths and weaknesses, and the buyers' needs and challenges, to formulate a plan that offers the greatest chance of success. It requires thinking several steps ahead and anticipating the obstacles you will encounter. Furthermore, it necessitates the ability to adapt your approach as needed to achieve your objectives.

Let's follow the example again of the data analysis company. They have seen a fall in demand for their product as buyers move to their competitors because of a new AI feature. The developers have said it will take six months to come even close to a similar feature in their product. As a seller, we have a decision to make. Do we jump ship as our product is going to die on the vine, or is there another plan that we can implement that drives value rather than competing on that specific feature? Can we find a way to reposition it so it's no longer important?

A strategic thinker is not reacting in the moment but considering the longer-term view and how they can adapt (that word again) the plan. Being too rigid in our approach can be just as detrimental as not having a plan at all. But the key is to strike a balance between being strategic and being flexible. A good plan is one that can adapt to chang-ing circumstances.

Again, think of it like a game of chess. You have a strategy going in. You know what your opponent's moves are likely to be, and you have a plan to counter them. But as the game progresses, things can change. Maybe your opponent makes an unexpected move. Maybe you realize that your plan isn't working as well as you'd hoped. The Infinite seller anticipates challenges, devises a plan of action and, most importantly, is agile.

Being a continuous learner

I have to admit to laughing about this one. As a company, Mentor Group gets paid to help peo-ple learn, so the potential conflict of interest of the attribute isn't lost on me! But do hear me out.

As a seller, your success depends on your ability to stay ahead. One of the best ways to do that is to be a continuous learner, whether that's ahead of the competition or ahead of the buyer.

Change is the only constant (I know a few physics professors who might argue with me, but you get the point!). New technologies emerge, preferences shift, and competitors come and go. If you wish to be suc-cessful as a seller, you need to keep up with these changes.

It means taking the time to educate yourself on the latest trends, technologies, and techniques. It could mean attending workshops, reading books, and networking with other sellers. It means being curious and asking questions. It means never being satisfied with the status quo.

Following our example, our product is now behind our competi-tors. They have implemented an innovative feature that uses AI to provide best-in-class visualization and insights. It's obvious that this is going to be a growth area, so you decide to act and learn more about the principles of AI, so that you can have a sensible conversation about what it actually means.

Maybe you attend a workshop. Maybe you read one of the many books on the topic. Maybe you reach out to other sellers on LinkedIn to ask for their advice. Whatever you do, you'll be taking steps to improve yourself and your business.

The most common objection to continuous learning is that it's hard to find the time and resources to do this regularly. This is true and can be done as part of your daily work. Even blocking one hour a week or 15 minutes per day, when done consistently, makes a powerful difference. Little and often is a very sustainable approach.

Being revenue-oriented

ORIENTATED

Well, this is stating the obvious. But is it?

I know we haven't completely covered this topic (go to Chapter 3 to dig in), but as we said in the intro, the future of selling is revenue, and revenue is the combination of all elements of the function that generates business. From lead generation to customer success, it's all about the revenue.

Therefore, we need to ensure that we don't have a myopic view of just being focused on sales but paying interest and being involved in the entire selling process.

The Infinite seller is interested in supporting everyone so that, collectively, we all (buyers too) achieve our goals. It is not just about the 'close' (although that is clearly important); it's about assuring we are oriented towards the bigger prize and, ultimately (see Chapter 4), making the pie bigger and supporting the buyers' goals.

Some people might argue that being revenue-oriented is a bad thing. They might say that it's not ethical or that it leads to shortsighted decision-making, but that's not what we are talking about here. We are not talking about a seller whose only thought is how they will win the deal and squeeze every bit of margin out of the buyers' hands. This is about supporting the philosophy of revenue rather than sales.

I don't want you to think I am against making money; it is the lifeblood of any business. Without money, you can't pay your bills, you can't pay your employees, and you can't invest in your business. It is what allows you to grow and expand.

When you're revenue-oriented, you're constantly thinking about providing your buyers with the best possible products and services that will enrich their organizations and help them to assist their customers. You're always looking for ways to improve and innovate. And that's the difference; it means that you're not just in it for the money – you're in it to make a difference.

It also forces you to be strategic. When you're focused on revenue, you're always looking for ways to maximize your impact. You're constantly analysing your sales data, looking for patterns and trends. You're testing different pricing strategies, experimenting with different marketing channels, and exploring new markets. You're always thinking about how you can get the most bang for your buck.

It means that you're not just winging it; you're making smart, data-driven decisions.

Being values-driven

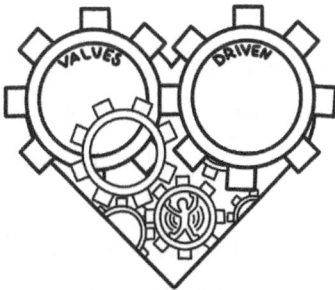

Finally, we get to being values-driven. This can be a bit of a cliché, but I have thought long and hard about whether or not to include it, as it can come across as a bit 'knit your own yoghurt'.

Being values-driven, in my mind, means that you have a set of core principles that guide everything you do. It means that you're not just here for the money; you're here to make a difference – a difference to the buyer, the market, your organization, and the humans that dwell in it.

When you're a values-driven seller, you're not just trying to sell something to someone. You're trying to create a relationship with them. You're trying to understand their needs and wants, and find a solution that works for them. And that's where integrity and authenticity come into play.

When you have integrity, you're honest and transparent with your buyers. You don't try to hide flaws in your product or oversell its benefits. Instead, you're upfront about what you're selling and what it can do. And that honesty creates trust with your buyers.

Similarly, you're not just putting on a show when you're authentic with your buyers. You're being yourself. You're showing your buyers who you are and what you stand for. And that authenticity creates a sense of connection with your buyers. They know that they're not just buying a product; they're buying from a person who cares about what they're selling.

Some people might argue that being values-driven, having integrity, and being authentic is a sure-fire way to lose sales. After all, isn't sales all about convincing people to buy something they might not need? If you think like that, please close this book now just in case I get you to change your mind (which I hope to).

Rather than values getting in the way, being values-driven, having integrity, and being authentic is essential for making sales.

When you're honest and transparent with your buyers, you build trust with them. They know that you're not just trying to sell them something – you're trying to help them. And that trust is invaluable when it comes to making a sale. When your buyers trust you, they're more likely to buy from you again in the future, and they're more likely to recommend you to others.

Similarly, when you're authentic with your buyers, you create a sense of connection with them. They know that they're not just dealing with a faceless organization; they're dealing with a person who cares about what they're selling. And that connection is invaluable when it comes to making a sale. When your buyers feel connected to you, they're more likely to buy from you, even if your competitors might be cheaper or have features you don't. Don't underestimate the power of trust.

Staying true to your values can be tough when you're pressured to make sales. But here's the thing: being values-driven, having integrity, and being authentic doesn't have to be at odds with making a profit.

In fact, I'd argue that the most successful sellers are those who are both values-driven and profitable. When you possess a clear set of values that guide everything you do, you have a strong sense of purpose. You understand why you're in this business and what you're working towards. That clarity of purpose is incredibly motivating.

It helps you to stay focused, even when things get tough. Have integrity. Be authentic. Don't be afraid to show your buyers who you are and what you stand for.

Attributes to actions

Table 1 gives a helpful summary of the Infinite seller attributes. It shows the skills we should have and the behaviour we would expect. But critically, there are also actions that demonstrate that the skills and behaviours are in place.

Without actions, these attributes become just nice things rather than a driving force of change that helps us support our buyers and create a new culture of selling.

Actions can also give us something else: measurement. As you will read in Chapter 8, measurement of change is vital and, as a lead indicator of success, sellers' actions are right at the top of the list!

What I hope is obvious is how different this table looks from previous seller attribute models. Rather than focusing on persuasion techniques and other softer skills, the Infinite seller attributes are much more about character and are focused on what really matters.

There is still huge value in soft skills, though, and these should still be demonstrable and teachable, but if the foundations are shaky, they will not make any difference.

Table 1   Infinite seller attributes

Attribute	Skills	Behaviours	Actions
Digitally literate	• Tech-savvy/ comfort • Data literate	• Can analyse and interpret data • Is willing to try new things to get the best results for the Buyer • Comfortable leading the way	• Used dashboards to gain insights • Adjusted strategy and responses based on data • Championed the use of new technologies as part of the Buyers solution
Buyer focused	• Empathy • Selflessness • Relational • Value creator	• Can put themselves in the shoes of the stakeholders • Effectively communicate across multiple modalities	• Used all modalities as required to communicate with Buyers and their stakeholders • Has adapted the value proposition and contextualized it for the Buyers world
Agile	• Decisiveness • Flexibility • Effectiveness • Resilience	• Can act decisively on information • Moves quickly and appropriately as needed • Is comfortable with change and ambiguity	• Has taken action quickly when required • Has changed strategy or course to better meet the needs of the Buyer

Table 1 (Continued)

Attribute	Skills	Behaviours	Actions
Strategic thinkers	• Innovative • Insightful • Creative • Analytical • Risk aware	• Has the ability to explore without judgement • Generates fresh perspectives and solutions • Develops and executes the digital Sales strategy • Aligns with both company and Buyer's mission Identifies and manages risks	• Has created a strategic account plan • Has completed the Buyer map • Has written thought leadership content • Has completed a risk assessment and risk mitigation plan
Continuous learners	• Growth mindset • Curiosity • Critical thinking • Initiative	• Is open-minded and enjoys experimenting with new thinking, tools and technologies • Actively seeks new opportunities to learn • Is consistent in their approach Goal setting	• Has completed some sort of training in the last 4 weeks • Has written thought leadership content • Has set clear goals for themselves and their accounts

(*Continued*)

Table 1   (Continued)

Attribute	Skills	Behaviours	Actions
Revenue-oriented	• Collaborative • Results focused • Financial acumen	• Is able to operate in an egoless manner • Is fully accountable for the results • Has an entrepreneurial attitude	• Has worked across the Infinite Loop with a buyer • Has reported on their goals with clarity • Has brought value to the wider team and to the buyer • Has negotiated a win–win
Values-driven	• Reflective • Ethical • Authentic	• Works with integrity with a byer-first attitude • Can operate with respect for the buyer, the company and their peers • Has the courage to operate to their values, even when difficult • Works on sustainable solutions for the buyers and company • Operates with transparency and clarity	• Has turned away business or opportunity as it does not fit their values • Has been transparent on the next steps with a buyer • Has developed a sustainable business/account plan

Remember, please take our free assessment at www.infiniteselling. com/attributes and see how you score. Just moving one of these attributes positively can significantly impact your effectiveness as a seller. You can take the assessment as often as you want to track your progress over time.

There is, however, one attribute I have not yet covered. I have not covered it as I believe it is *the* foundation of all the other attributes. It is so important I have dedicated an entire chapter to it: mental fitness.

Chapter 2

Mental fitness: The foundation of sales performance

Build your core

In the introduction, we started to discuss a concept that is largely unspoken about in the selling community but is something that impacts us all daily. It is possible that this issue is the largest contributor to lost sales and productivity globally. It is, in Matt's and my opinion, the single largest opportunity to improve selling performance, and the biggest catalyst for change.

I am, of course, talking about mental fitness.

Let's look at some of the research on the impact of mental fitness:

- Research from the Centre for Mental Health (Centre for Mental Health, 2024) reveals that the total cost of mental ill health in England in 2022 was £300 billion, comprising economic costs (£110 billion), human costs (£130 billion), and health and care costs (£60 billion).
- According to Deloitte and Meharry Medical College research (Deloitte, 2024), excess costs arising from mental health inequities total an estimated US$477.5 billion in 2024, with projections suggesting this could exceed US$1.3 trillion by 2040.
- McKinsey Health Institute research (McKinsey Health Institute, 2025) indicates that scaling known, cost-effective mental health interventions could unlock US$4.4 trillion in global GDP by 2050, with each US$1 invested potentially generating an economic return of US$5 to US$6.

- Deloitte's Health Equity Institute (Deloitte, 2024) projects that, if left unaddressed, mental health inequities could lead to approximately US$14 trillion in excess costs between now and 2040.

Just let the information in this list sink in. What would be the impact if we could change these by just a few per cent? You don't need to get a calculator out to know that the changes to our results could be truly transformational. So why is there still such a big issue if there is so much benefit and potential? Quite simply because we don't talk about it. It gets pushed under the carpet and ignored.

Selling can be – and this is something that must change – a hostile environment. It is full of toxic behaviours and attitudes, which are driving unprecedented pressure on sellers. They must hit targets and, if they do, they are rewarded with a higher target, which adds more stress and creates a vicious circle that becomes incredibly hard to break.

Seller teams often meet weekly, where their performance number is scrutinized by others, frequently publicly with their peers.

This would be okay if there were a supportive culture, but when this is coupled with a performance culture that only values bottom-line results, this heaps on even more pressure.

Is it any wonder that employee turnover in selling is so high?

It's easy to say something clichéd like, 'If you can't stand the heat…', but that's a very unhelpful and incredibly naive approach as it's missing the point entirely. Let me expand.

Attraction and retention of talent are one of, if not the biggest, single issues facing organizations today. This is not a new issue that has seen many talented people review what is important to them and either drop off the workplace altogether or change careers. The net impact is that we have less talent. Experience is walking out the door mainly because the work environments presented to them are no longer seen as valuable.

Considering that, according to McKinsey and Company (McKinsey & Company, 2021), the cost of replacing a seller is at least five times the quota of the seller who left, we are facing a serious and significant problem. Just think about what that truly means. If someone departs with a £200,000 target, it will cost you £1 million to replace them. Ouch.

With some investment and focus, however, we can change this. We can make our sellers' environments attractive again. And this cannot simply be achieved with money anymore. Gone are the days when throwing money at sellers would persuade them to overlook poor, toxic, and damaging working practices.

We can see this where sellers are choosing to give up well-paying roles for a career that isn't so toxic, but also because the next generation is not motivated by the money anymore. They are motivated by their values.

These values differ significantly from those of the current generation, with common values including a desire for:

- work–life balance;
- a sense of purpose;
- flexibility; and
- a commitment to diversity and inclusion.

Did you notice that money was missing from this list?

The next generation wants a different workplace, and so, if we fail to adapt, not only are we going to lose (and have already lost) talent, but we are also going to struggle to recruit new talent as the brightest stars will migrate to workplaces that are more in line with their values.

I truly believe that dealing with mental fitness in sales, along with flexible working, will become a competitive differentiator. Organizations that embrace it and put in programmes specifically to help improve seller mental fitness will not only attract and retain better talent, but the evidence also shows (as you will see later in the chapter) that they outperform other organizations in every metric.

So, how do you know how mentally fit you are? Well, there are plenty of tools that you can use to find this out, but here is a simple litmus test. If you have experienced or are experiencing any of the following, there is a chance there is work to do on your mental fitness:

- You are regularly overwhelmed by self-doubt.
- You struggle to bounce back from hardship.
- You often feel on the edge of burnout.
- You find it difficult to manage stress and anxiety.
- You struggle with a lack of focus.
- You get side-tracked by failures.
- There is often conflict in relationships.
- You experience communication breakdowns regularly.

My guess is that we have all experienced at least one of these. And that's good news as it means we are all in the same boat. No stigma. We *all* have issues with our mental health from time to time and there is no shame in admitting it.

When we realize others are in the same boat, we can start to use our empathy to change the workplace and to create high trust, which in turn creates high performance.

But there is another benefit. Flexing our empathy muscle for our colleagues also helps us to learn empathy for our clients. This a top skill for any seller as it allows us to truly understand the buyer and ensure we help to align our value propositions directly to their need.

Again, this is not new. Every book on sales I have ever read discusses the need for empathy. But not a single one has suggested how to build empathy as a skill. So, let's address that.

Empathy, with some exceptions, is a skill we all have. For some people, like Matt, it comes naturally. Matt is naturally warm and seems to have an intuition about how someone may feel and how to meet it.

I, on the other hand, have had to learn it. I can be incredibly data-driven and have, in the past, focused on that data far more than on people. It's got me into much trouble. But it also drove me to learn how to be empathetic, which was developed by watching others and experiencing empathy from others.

The latter point is more important than you might think. By experiencing empathy *from* others, we learn how it makes us feel, and thus we can appreciate how it must feel for others and, eventually, how to show empathy to others and – here's the rub – ourselves.

The ability to be naturally empathetic, or someone who must learn to be, is polarizing – especially as, ironically, we struggle to understand each other's worlds. However, both sides can understand (again, with some exceptions) that we need to have empathy for ourselves as well.

Despite understanding that we can empathize with ourselves, we often don't permit ourselves to do it. The net impact of not having empathy for yourself is that you start to spiral. There is a tendency to blame yourself or others for your mistakes and, as a result, fail to take ownership, leaving you out of control.

Creating an empathetic workplace that supports and even develops mental fitness for yourself and for your peers is going to be a key driver of success for you personally and for your organization.

Mental fitness or mental health

But why am I talking about mental fitness rather than mental health? Mental health is today's hot topic, right? The reason is, mental health is a lagging indicator of your mental fitness, much like your physical health; it is impacted by how well you physically exercise.

By focusing on mental fitness, we focus on something we can change; something we can influence on a daily, if not hourly, basis. It is under our control.

Just like regular physical exercise will, over time, impact our physical health, we can do mental exercises that will, over time, impact our mental health.

The even better news is that it doesn't even need to be hard. We just need to do it regularly, and then we can let our amazing physiology do the rest.

As an organization, Mentor Group has been working closely with Positive Intelligence, an organization at the forefront of the mental fitness movement. Their founder and CEO, Shirzad Chamine, is a passionate advocate of the importance and impact mental fitness can have on an individual, and their groundbreaking PQ programme has shown just how much a positive change in mental fitness can impact sales. Here is what some other PQ clients saw:

- 37% of salespeople outsold the control group (global healthcare)
- 93% increase in productivity (global communications)
- 34% profit growth (UK hospitality)
- 32% increase in booked sales (CIBC)
- 71% increase in pipeline (CIBC)
- US$55,200 more sales per seller per month (pharma), and
- US$91,370 more sales per seller per month (health and beauty).

Get your calculator out. Work out what it means to you and your business if you were able to get results like those in this list. It would not be evolutionary; it would be transformational. And yet not one selling skill was taught. It was all about how we behave and respond to the world around us.

The PQ programme focuses on the concept that we all have saboteurs. These saboteurs have been built by us, over time, to help and protect us, but they sabotage our success.

They include:

- a desire to control everything and everyone (my personal sab);
- the need to please others to avoid conflict and to be seen as the nice one;

- a preference to avoid difficult conversations or decisions; and
- needing to have *all* the facts before doing anything.

There are nine of them in total, and I would heartily recommend you read the book *Positive Intelligence* (Chamine, 2012) and even take the free Saboteur Assessment (www.positiveintelligence.com/saboteurs/) to understand each fully.

The point is that we all have things in our lives that can either help or hinder us, but until we are mentally fit enough to work through these, we will always be subject to the limited thinking and negative impacts that these saboteurs can bring.

Again, these saboteurs originated for good reasons, but as the famous saying goes, 'What got us here is not going to get us there', so we need to be brave enough to work through them; even better is that we work through them together, as the extension of knowing your saboteurs is knowing those of others you work with – again, developing empathy to understand where they are coming from and how best to communicate with them.

I am sure the astute among you can see that the even further extension of this is knowing your buyers' saboteurs, but that's another book entirely.

Selling is a challenging profession that, as we have explained earlier, requires a high degree of mental fitness. Our day-to-day roles involve dealing with rejection, handling objections, and maintaining a positive attitude in the face of adversity.

It's not easy but well worth it. For completeness (and for my need to reinforce the point), let's now look at five other benefits of strong mental fitness in selling.

Improved focus and concentration

Mental fitness can help sellers maintain focus and concentration, even in high-pressure situations. Mentally fit sellers can stay engaged during long meetings, make quick decisions, and adapt to changing circumstances. This is supported by a study conducted by the National Institutes of Health, which found that mental training can improve focus and attention span in sellers.

Better emotional control

Another study, this time published in the *Journal of Business and Psychology* (2016), found that emotional intelligence is positively associated with selling performance. It showed that emotional control is crucial in selling because it allows sellers to maintain a positive attitude, even in the face of rejection. A mentally fit seller can handle negative feedback and objections without becoming defensive or aggressive. They can keep their emotions in check and use them to connect with buyers meaningfully.

Improved creativity

Mental fitness can improve creativity in sellers. That's a bold statement, but the *Journal of Marketing Research* (2022) found that creative thinking is positively associated with selling performance. As we all know, selling requires constant innovation, and a mentally fit seller can come up with new and creative solutions to problems. They can think outside the box and find unique ways to connect with their buyers.

Better customer relationship management

The *Harvard Business Review* (2015) found that emotional intelligence is critical in customer relationship management. A mentally fit seller can build strong connections with buyers, understand their needs, and provide personalized solutions. They can use their emotional intelligence to build rapport and trust with buyers. People buy from people, so rapport and trust are both essential.

Increased resilience

Resilience is the ability to bounce back from setbacks and challenges. Selling can be a tough business, and rejection is a common occurrence. A mentally fit seller can bounce back from rejections and setbacks quickly and keep moving forward. They can maintain a positive outlook and keep their focus on their goals.

Mental resilience = revenue resilience.

If we can keep our mentality resilient, we are in a better position to maintain our selling performance, which, of course, impacts the only measurement that really matters – revenue realization.

And it really does go beyond just an individual seller; the whole revenue organization must take it on. It's no good for us all to be enlightened sellers when the manager is not. Meetings will have a mismatched feel and the possibility to descend into negativity, resulting in a dysfunctional team, poor performance and, ultimately, high staff turnover.

We need to get into a place of flow: ease and flow. If we can sense that we are not, it should be a yellow flag that something is wrong.

Flow state, also known as being 'in the zone', is a mental state where we are fully immersed in a task, feeling energized, focused, and enjoying the process. Being in a flow state is critical for sellers and leaders, as it can do wonders for our collective performance, creativity, and productivity.

As I said earlier, sellers often face challenges in work (rejection, competition, stress, etc.), leading to the dreaded burnout and decreased daily motivation.

However, being in a flow state can help us to overcome these challenges and achieve our goals, because when we are in a true flow state, we are better able to handle the rejections, more resilient in the face of setbacks, more creative in our approaches to selling, and are more likely to come up with innovative solutions to problems.

Ultimately, being in flow can lead to increased productivity. We can complete tasks faster and with fewer errors because we are fully focused on the task at hand, not the mind's distractions. As a result, we can accomplish more in less time, which benefits us all.

Managers will also benefit as effective management, which requires fun tasks like setting goals, developing strategies, and motivating the team, can better handle the pressure and stress associated with the job when everyone is in flow. They are better able to make decisions quickly, develop creative strategies, and communicate effectively with the team.

For managers, being in flow can enhance leadership skills, as the individual is more focused on the present moment and can connect with their team members on a deeper level. This can improve team morale, increase motivation, and create a more positive work environment.

As I mentioned at the start of this chapter, mental fitness is vital for success in selling. When strong, a mentally fit seller can effortlessly tackle sales challenges and realize their full potential. Investing in mental fitness can elevate your career to the next level and lead to lasting success.

Okay, I think I have made my point. But how exactly do you do it?

Make mental fitness the centre of your selling skills

Putting mental fitness into your daily life isn't hard. I am not saying it doesn't take effort, but it is not hard. It is more about making it a habit.

Software applications and mindfulness programs, like the Positive Intelligence PQ program, can provide you with a set of daily activities and even a mental fitness gym that guides you through simple mindfulness exercises that can be done anywhere and at any time, making it convenient and fun to build a habit.

They know that creating small habits that are done regularly builds great strength, just like press-ups (full disclosure, I hate press-ups) or sit-ups. Do them daily, and you will see a difference. The trick is to find something that works for you. The mistake is to think there is one size that fits all. Find what works for you. Something that fits into your day helps to ground you and bring you back to a place where you can deal with what's in front of you.

One of the things that really helped me is learning about my natural circadian rhythm and ensuring that I follow that as much as possible. For those unaware, your circadian rhythm is your internal biological clock that regulates various physiological processes. This includes the sleep–wake cycle, body temperature, hormone secretion, and metabolism.

The impact of the circadian rhythm on our health and well-being is significant. Disruptions to our circadian rhythm, such as those caused by stress, jet lag, or irregular sleep patterns, can lead to various health problems, including sleep disorders, metabolic disorders, cardiovascular disease, and mood disorders. It also manages how energized we are at certain times of the day and even how creative we can be.

What's truly important is recognizing that mental fitness is as important as physical fitness, and then giving it the same attention, focus, and discipline.

Like any new habit, start small, and as small as you like. Just do it regularly to build muscle memory, and soon you will fly. Our work with sellers in this area is profound, and the impact is almost immediate and gets even better with time as you become stronger and stronger.

If you want to really drive up your game, learning how to create successful habits is a critical skill, and there is no better book to read on that subject than *Atomic Habits* by James Clear (2018). Trust me, it's worth reading every word.

Talk about it

As mentioned earlier, the biggest challenge with the topic of mental fitness is talking about it. Or, to be specific, not talking about it.

While the stigma is reducing as awareness is increasing, in some work cultures it is still there. Where it is still a taboo, anything with the word 'mental' before it seems to get labelled as a weakness. But nothing is further from the truth. Those people who can talk about mental health and manage their mental fitness have the best outcomes and will deliver the best results.

That's why, in our work with clients, we often build deliberate discussion areas into the regular cadence of meetings. Whether it is a one-to-one with your manager or a group call, some element of mental fitness is always happening as a specific agenda item. For example, in any group session, having a 5-minute agenda item for people to call out what they are grateful for (work or personal) is an incredibly powerful way to start a meeting. This simple discipline changes the atmosphere of the meeting. It literally changes the energy and helps to ensure the meeting runs with positivity.

Is it awkward at first? Of course it is. But over time, it generates a culture that is the perfect fertilizer for a high-performing team.

I have seen teams that used to be in conflict every meeting, come together, bond, and then perform by just adding this simple 5-minute addition to the agenda.

Another area we encourage is celebration, to celebrate the successes of everyone in a meaningful way. As a culture (remember, Matt and I are British, so stoicism is built in at birth), we aren't great at celebrating the little wins, but it makes a real difference when you celebrate in the meeting. It's easy to overlook this, but our experience is that when something is celebrated, it is repeated.

We also encourage talking about mental fitness and sharing what has worked (or not) as part of our learning hub meeting. This critical part of the revenue velocity accelerator is where sellers get together to share best practices. This is normally dominated by topics such as sales skills or product knowledge, but using it to drive a conversation around mental fitness is powerful.

For example, here are some conversation starters that can be used in a learning hub.

1) How do you prioritize your mental health and well-being in your daily routine?
2) What are some of your go-to strategies for managing stress and anxiety?
3) Have you ever tried mindfulness or meditation? If so, how has it impacted your mental health?
4) What role does exercise play in your mental health and well-being?
5) How do you stay motivated and inspired when facing mental health challenges?

Talking about mental fitness may be uncomfortable for many, and it will require a shift in mentality from us, both as individuals and in company culture. Still, in our experience and the tangible results we have seen with our clients, no other skill can have such a deep and profound change in an organization.

In conclusion, focusing on mental fitness in sales should be a total no-brainer. Let's do a quick recap.

✓ It's a competitive differentiator to attracting new talent.
✓ It reduces employee attrition and the cost of replacement (average of 5x their quota).
✓ It improves productivity.
✓ It improves pipeline.
✓ It improves booked sales.
✓ It improves profit.

Still think it's a topic best left to HR? Get this foundation right, and the sky is the limit, not just for sellers but for the organization as a whole.

Chapter 3

Revenue, not sales

Sales is dead, long live revenue

Matt and I have been in the sales business for the last 30 years, from doing the hard work looking for leads, to enterprise account management, to finally managing entire teams. Mentor Group itself has built its reputation around sales training, enablement, transformation, and consultancy.

It would not be an exaggeration to say that our whole careers have revolved around the word 'sales' in one way, shape, or form.

But there is a natural order of life, and there is a time when everything needs to die and be superseded, and, for Matt and me, it's time for sales to die.

That's a dangerous thing to say, especially given that our target audience for the book is people in sales. But this is also not new thinking. There has been a movement over the last few years, from conversations on sales to conversations around revenue. We see more CROs (Chief Revenue Officers) than CSOs (Chief Sales Officers). Gartner is starting to talk about revenue intelligence as a sector (Gartner, n.d.), and you can't move without someone writing a blog on 'the rise of revenue'. And for very good reason.

Revenue is ultimately what any organization should be focused on. It is the outcome of the collective effort of many parts of the organization. It is the only metric that really matters.

So, what does it mean to be revenue-oriented?

Most agree that being revenue-oriented means taking a more holistic approach to revenue generation. Instead of solely focusing on the sales department, a revenue-oriented approach considers all the different activities and departments contributing to generating revenue. This includes marketing, customer success, product development, support, HR, etc.

At a high level, there are several reasons why being revenue-oriented is so important for our organizational health and the long-term success of all involved, as the following explains.

It takes into account all revenue-generating activities

By being revenue-oriented, organizations can identify opportunities to improve revenue growth in all areas, not just sales. For example, marketing campaigns can be optimized to generate higher-quality leads, and customer success teams can be trained to upsell and renew existing customers. By taking a holistic approach, organizations can look to maximize their revenue growth opportunities across the customer lifecycle.

It promotes collaboration and alignment

When a company mainly focuses on sales, it can create a siloed environment where the sales team is solely responsible for generating revenue. This can create tension and a lack of collaboration with the other departments. By taking a revenue-oriented approach, all departments are seen as contributors to revenue growth, which can lead to a more collaborative and results-driven culture.

It allows for a data-driven approach

A revenue-oriented approach allows companies to analyse data across all revenue-generating departments. This can identify trends and opportunities that a sales-focused approach may have missed. For example, data may show that a specific marketing campaign generates high-quality leads that are more likely to result in sales. This information can be used to make informed decisions about where to invest resources and how to optimize revenue generation. This, of course, is getting further enhanced by AI, which is showing great promise in how it can analyse disparate data sets to give very powerful insights.

It promotes long-term sustainability

While sales are important for generating revenue in the short term, a company solely focused on sales may struggle to sustain revenue growth over time. A revenue-oriented approach considers the company's long-term health, including factors such as retention, product development, and brand reputation.

Given the important benefits, which should be obvious from the text you have just read, it's no wonder the role of the CRO is such a focus area. So, there begs the question: If the benefits are so obvious and the impact so large, why isn't everyone doing it? Why isn't everyone clamouring to change their focus from sales to revenue? This is not an easy question to answer, mainly because it can fall into many areas, but here are a few of the current blockers:

- **Siloed departments (the biggest and most obvious!):** Many organizations have separate sales, marketing, and customer success teams that operate independently, making it difficult to coordinate efforts and adopt a revenue-oriented approach.
- **Limited technology:** Organizations may lack the necessary technology infrastructure to support a revenue-oriented strategy, such as a unified CRM system, automated workflows, and real-time data analytics.
- **Inflexible processes:** Organizations may be resistant to change and may have rigid processes that are difficult to modify, making it challenging to adopt new revenue-oriented strategies.
- **Limited resources:** Implementing a revenue-oriented strategy requires resources such as dedicated personnel, technology,

and training, which can be difficult to secure in resource-constrained organizations.

- **Cultural resistance:** Sales teams might resist change and feel threatened by the notion of a CRO or revenue-oriented strategy, especially if they believe it could adversely affect their compensation or role.
- **Lack of leadership support:** Implementing a revenue-oriented strategy can be challenging without buy-in from senior leadership, as it requires significant organizational and cultural changes.

While the issue of siloed departments may be the biggest and obvious blocker, it is the last two – cultural resistance and lack of leadership support – that are the real blockers and the real key to this.

One for all

When we deploy our sales management system, there is a reason we start with the sales leaders. We know that without them and their support, we will not get the transformation we need, as they will not be engaged or even believe in what we are doing.

Without top-down alignment, nothing will stick, and you end up with just another initiative.

The concept of revenue versus sales has the same issue. Change cannot be affected without top-down buy-in that there needs to be wholesale change that must start with the most senior leaders.

When examining control groups with engaged leaders, in contrast to those with leaders who are not fully onboard, we observe increased performance across every sales metric. From productivity to profit, achieving alignment throughout the organization is crucial.

So why do some managers, when they can see the evidence, still not buy in?

There are several complex reasons, but they can be summarized into two pots: pride, or insecurity. I understand that this may come across as somewhat harsh, but given the hard numbers demonstrating the benefits and my belief that people generally wish to do the right thing, it is a reasonable conclusion.

Pride

One of my odd interests is looking at the impact of pride across human history. It seems so obvious that a large proportion of the world's troubles comes from pride as a root cause. Whether that be wars or negotiation failure, track it back, and pride is at the core.

Throughout history, pride has caused conflicts between individuals and even entire nations. When people are too proud to admit they're wrong or compromise, it can lead to arguments, misunderstandings, and even wars. I am sure we can all think of examples, both in history and probably in our own lives.

Pride can also lead to discrimination and prejudice. When people are so proud of their own thinking that they believe it is superior to others, they may discriminate against those who are different. Again, I would wager we can all think of examples of that too.

Another impact is that pride can also prevent progress and hinder innovation. When people are too proud to admit they don't know something or need help, they may refuse to seek out new knowledge or collaborate with others. This can lead to stagnation and a lack of growth. From my own experience (and shame), I held on to beliefs that hindered my growth and the growth of the people I was leading.

It can blind people to the reality of their situation. When someone is too proud to admit they're wrong or that they need help, they may continue down a path that is ultimately destructive. This can lead to a lot of unnecessary suffering and hardship for themselves and others around them.

One of the more insidious impacts of pride can also lead to a lack of empathy and compassion. When someone is so focused on their own accomplishments and status, they may not be able to relate to or understand the struggles of others. This can lead to a lack of support for those who need it and a lack of understanding and unity in society.

I believe this latter point significantly impacts sales leaders, especially as most of them have arrived at their destination through hard work, fighting in the trenches of sales. They believe that if they had to do it, so must you. This is hugely limiting and potentially destructive.

While pride can be a positive trait when kept in check, excessive pride can be incredibly destructive. It can lead to conflicts, discrimination, and a lack of progress and personal growth. By practising humility and empathy, and celebrating diversity, we can combat excessive pride and create a more compassionate and inclusive society.

Did you notice the link there between how we can combat pride and the attributes of an Infinite seller? I don't want to come across as preachy, but this is a passion area, and I wanted to ensure this was a core pillar in this work.

Insecurity

Being a sales leader can be a high-pressure role, and it's natural to feel some insecurity now and then. However, when insecurity becomes a dominant force in a sales leader's life, it can negatively affect the team and the business as a whole.

One of the biggest problems with insecurity in sales leadership (and other leadership types, too, to be fair) is that it can lead to micromanagement.

When a sales leader feels insecure about their abilities, they may feel the need to control every aspect of their team's work to ensure that everything is done 'right'. However, this level of micromanagement can be incredibly demotivating for team members, who may feel that they aren't trusted to perform their jobs.

Insecurity can also lead to a lack of confidence in decision-making. When a sales leader feels unsure of themselves, they may hesitate to make important decisions or take risks. This can lead to missed opportunities and a lack of innovation, harming the business's success.

It can also lead to a lack of accountability. When a sales leader feels insecure, they may be reluctant to hold their team members accountable for their actions. This can create a culture of complacency and can lead to a lack of motivation and performance within the team. Worse, it can create a culture of blame, where the leader is looking to find others to pin their failings on, and often that is either the sellers or the marketers.

Insecurity can also create a toxic work environment. When a sales leader feels insecure, they may be prone to lashing out at their team members or being overly critical of their work. This can create a culture of fear and can make it difficult for team members to feel valued and appreciated.

This often boils over into sales meetings, where the leader is driven by their own behaviour to scrutinize and criticize their sellers. They lose their perspective.

While it's natural to feel some insecurity as a sales leader, it's important to recognize the negative impact that it can have on the team and the business.

It is one of the reasons that mental fitness features so strongly in the INFINITE method, as with strong mental fitness, insecurities fade, and you can start to operate free of the saboteurs that may be holding you and your company back.

The truth about CROs

Hopefully, you can see from this discussion why the two pots of pride and insecurity are the underlying blockers for putting in a revenue model. It is not that sales leaders can't do it; it is just that they are protecting themselves from risk.

But we need to be brave enough to make a change, to embrace a truly integrated team, one that works together as a seamless organism focused on revenue. And this is the real differentiator and the absolute key to success – ONE team.

The truth is that most CROs are still running two teams. They are running a sales team and a marketing team. Both teams just report to one leader (CRO). I must admit that this is a good first step in the right direction and it is better than having two totally separate silos, but they are still siloed and are not in step with each other.

Sure, there are probably 'sales and marketing interlocks' or joint initiatives, but they still operate as two departments at the end of the day.

What needs to happen is a paradigm shift in thinking. We need to stop thinking of ourselves as sales and marketing. We are all in this together, and there is so much power in combining the skills of marketeers with sales and a much deeper level. As the musketeers would say: 'One for all, and all for one.'

The Infinite motion

We chose the term 'Infinite motion' deliberately as it captures the essential truth that selling is no longer a process with a clear beginning and end. Traditional thinking treats sales like a relay race: marketing generates a lead, passes it to sales, sales converts it, then hands it off to customer success.

This linear approach is not just outdated – it's actively damaging your business.

The reality is far more sophisticated. Selling resembles a continuous dance where every participant must stay in rhythm throughout the entire performance. When executed properly, this coordination creates something genuinely elegant. When done poorly, it becomes a disaster where departments step on each other's toes, fight for the lead, and operate with their eyes shut to what's actually happening around them.

The visual representation of this concept shows a continuous loop rather than a linear process. Instead of viewing the purchase as the endpoint, it sits at the centre of ongoing activity.

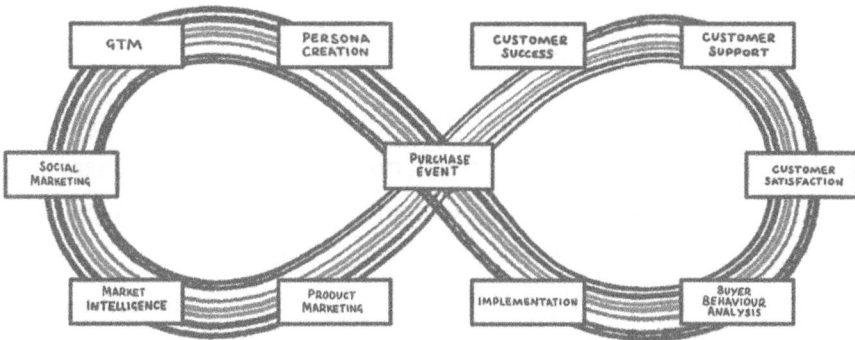

Everything before the purchase focuses on attracting buyers; everything after focuses on retaining and expanding those relationships. This buyer-focused approach never stops.

The data that demands action

Two statistics from Gartner should terrify every sales leader still operating under old assumptions:

- Some 61% of buyers want a rep-free experience (Gartner, 2025a).
- Customers spend only 17% of their buying journey interacting with sales teams (Gartner, 2021).

These figures aren't suggestions; they're a declaration that buyer behaviour has permanently shifted.

Yet most organizations continue investing the majority of their enablement budget in areas that influence less than one-fifth of the buyer's journey. This misallocation of resources explains why so many sales teams struggle despite working harder than ever.

The implications are stark. If buyers actively avoid sales interactions and conduct 83% of their journey independently, then organizations must excel at answering questions before buyers know they need to ask them. This represents a complete reversal of traditional sales methodology.

The question revolution

For decades, sales training focused on teaching representatives how to ask brilliant questions. This approach made sense when the sellers controlled information access and buyers depended on sales interactions for product knowledge. Those days are over permanently.

The new reality demands that organizations become exceptional at answering questions rather than asking them. Buyers now arrive at sales conversations already informed – or they don't arrive at all. If your content, website, and digital presence fail to address their concerns comprehensively, they simply move to competitors who do.

This shift requires organizations to anticipate buyer questions and provide answers across all touchpoints before any sales interaction occurs. The challenge is significant: you cannot adapt your message in real-time when the buyer has already moved on to other options.

Why this changes everything

The power dynamic has irreversibly shifted from sellers to buyers. Buyers possess all the information they need to make informed purchasing decisions. If that information isn't readily available from your organization, they eliminate you from consideration without ever speaking to your sales team.

This transformation affects every aspect of how businesses should operate, as the following outlines.

- **Resource allocation:** Continuing to invest primarily in sales training while ignoring the 83% of the buyer journey that happens without sales involvement is strategic malpractice.

- **Content strategy:** Every piece of content must anticipate and answer buyer questions comprehensively, as you won't get a second chance to clarify or expand your message.
- **Team collaboration:** The artificial boundaries between marketing, sales, and customer success must disappear. The motion is continuous, and everyone must own the entire cycle.
- **Measurement systems:** Focusing solely on sales metrics while ignoring earlier and later stages of the buyer journey provides an incomplete and misleading picture of performance.

The new role of sales

This evolution doesn't eliminate the need for sales professionals; it transforms their function entirely. Modern sellers must become value engineers who demonstrate both tangible and intangible benefits while influencing the 95% to sell to the 5%. This approach produces better-qualified prospects and improves every critical sales metric.

The traditional focus on closing deals creates short-term, seller-focused behaviours that often conflict with organizational and buyer objectives. We've all witnessed deals completed purely to benefit the salesperson despite negative impacts on broader relationships and outcomes.

The competitive advantage

Organizations that embrace this Infinite motion approach gain several critical advantages.

- **Better qualified prospects:** When buyers self-educate using your content and reach sales conversations already convinced of your value, conversion rates and deal sizes increase significantly.

- **Reduced sales cycles.** Educated buyers make decisions faster because they've already completed much of their evaluation process.
- **Higher customer satisfaction:** Buyers who thoroughly understand your offering before purchasing experience fewer surprises and greater satisfaction.
- **Competitive protection:** Comprehensive digital presence and content strategy make it harder for competitors to displace your solutions.

Implementation reality

The statistics about digital-first selling represent a permanent shift, not a temporary trend. While some argue that complex deals still require human interaction or that the pendulum swings will restore traditional selling, these perspectives miss the fundamental change in buyer expectations and capabilities.

Complex deal thresholds continue rising as buyers become comfortable making larger purchases digitally. Even when trends do reverse, each cycle reduces the impact of traditional approaches, making them niche rather than mainstream strategies.

The path forward

Organizations must stop treating this as a sales or marketing problem. It's a business problem requiring coordinated action across all customer-facing functions. The Infinite motion demands that every team member understand and own the entire buyer journey rather than focusing on isolated segments.

Success requires answering buyer questions before they're asked, demonstrating value before relationships begin, and maintaining engagement long after purchases are complete. This approach transforms episodic transactions into continuous partnerships that drive sustained growth and competitive advantage.

The choice is simple: evolve your approach to match how buyers actually behave, or watch them consistently choose competitors who do.

Grit or quit

Early in my sales career, I was given one piece of advice, which has stuck with me and is something I believe to be still true today. That advice was that good people qualify 'in' (trying to justify why the deal should happen), while great people qualify 'out' (trying to persuade themselves that there is no deal and to move on).

I have used this as a guiding light and have always tried to approach all my selling in that way, and I have encouraged many sellers and leaders to do the same, but it is not always well received.

Let's cover some basics.

Qualifying opportunities in sales is like the bread and butter of selling. Or you could consider it more like salt and pepper, the essential seasoning that makes the dish come together.

But what exactly does it mean to qualify an opportunity? It's about determining whether a potential buyer is a good fit for your product or service.

Do they have a need that your offering can address? Do they have the budget to pay for it? Do they have the decision-making authority to make the purchase?

It's not just about ensuring the buyer is a good fit for you. It's also about ensuring you're a good fit for them. After all, you don't want to waste your time (or theirs) trying to sell them something they don't need or want.

This latter point is why qualifying out is such an important skill. It can save you a lot of time and effort. If you spend all your energy trying to sell to someone who's not a good fit, you're wasting your time and missing out on other potential buyers who might be a better match for your product or service.

Qualifying out can also help you to maintain your reputation and credibility. If you try to sell to someone who's not a good fit and they have a bad experience, they're likely to tell others about it. Word of mouth is powerful, and a few negative reviews can do much damage to your business.

In any sales training, there is always some section on qualification. Here are a few of the most popular.

- **BANT:** As mentioned earlier, BANT stands for Budget, Authority, Need, and Timeline.
- **MEDDIC:** This methodology stands for Metrics, Economic Buyer, Decision Criteria, Decision Process, Identify Pain, and Champion. Note: MEDDIC has now been largely replaced with MEDDPIC which includes an additional P standing for Paper Process. Don't get distracted about the Paper part; it's there to point out that we need to understand the seller process to buy.
- **SPIN selling:** SPIN stands for Situation, Problem, Implication, and Need-Payoff. This methodology helps salespeople to uncover the prospect's situation, identify the problem they are facing, explore the implications of not solving it, and finally, present a solution that delivers a need-payoff.

Essentially, these pose the same question, regardless of the perspective. They ensure that as a seller, we thoroughly comprehend the transaction and are mindful of all the relevant components.

Used correctly – and as I have said, for me, that's qualifying out, not in – they all have their place. BANT, for example, is a great litmus test. It's quick, unrefined, but extremely effective.

MEDDIC (or MEDDPIC, or any other number of variations of this model) is far more nuanced and can be extremely effective in finding the important edges of a deal.

The trick is not the methodology used but rather having the mental fitness and ability to say no. The skill is knowing when to quit (qualify out) or have grit (stick with it and qualify in).

All that these methodologies do is give you data. They give you markers and pointers on what the next step may be. Put in a process, they are gates. If all gates are open, continue. If they are closed, don't do it.

An emotionless selling process is a very, very powerful tool and one that all sellers should embrace. But there is a shadow. And that shadow is down to us and our ability to interpret the data correctly. Let me explain.

If you are a typical seller within a typical organization, you are facing significant pressure. You are confronted with targets, your actions are measured more than in any other role I know, and even your behaviours are scrutinized by various technologies that distil your work into a series of numbers.

You are behind on your numbers when, unexpectedly, an opportunity arises that seems likely to bridge the gap. Although you have some reservations, it promises to cover the shortfall. Your leader will ease off your back for five minutes to allow you some breathing space.

You qualify in. Why? Not because the data says so, but rather to relieve yourself, to have some hope.

But it doesn't always work when you are behind your number. It also happens when you are ahead of target, and the company believes it's a great idea to put accelerators into your compensation plan. Of course, you want this deal to go ahead. What have you got to lose? You are already ahead of target. This is the icing on the cake and will get you a place in the president's club. Again, you qualify in.

In truth, there is no skill in qualification. Every methodology (and Infinite is not really any different in this regard) has a set of questions to ask that will give you the answers. Apply these in the right order and at the right time (there is a little skill in that, to be fair, but that's more about how we say something rather than what to say), and you will get the right result.

The skill is in being strong enough to say no and being strong enough to stay with it. This is where the magic happens, the differentiator between the good and the great.

There is an old film (1992 is old in my book) called *Glengarry Glen Ross*, starring Al Pacino, Jack Lemmon, and Alec Baldwin, to name but a few. In it, they do some teaching with Mr Baldwin, and while very old-school in the approach (not to mention deceitful and dubious), they are taught ABC: 'Always be closing.'

It's easy to remember and had its merits back in the day, but ABC needs to move to ABV for this century: 'Always be validating.' Not quite as catchy, I know, but it should still be memorable.

At every opportunity, after every interaction, you should be critically asking yourself: From the data I have, do I quit or have grit?

This is the most important question in selling. Get it right and it will transform your selling and your team's performance as they focus on the right deals, with more time working on a reality that will happen. Get it wrong and you will be spinning your wheels.

Remember, in selling, particularly now, our job is to influence the 95% and sell to the 5% – focus and clarity. Done right, influence is simply the product of awareness + resonance.

Importance of influence

Let me start by saying how much I dislike this word. I dislike this word nearly as much as someone describing themselves as a sherpa (you'll hear more about that in later chapters!). Of course, there is nothing wrong with the word itself as it accurately describes the action. It is just what else it conjures up.

Influence can be seen as manipulative or bringing up memories of Insta filters and odd dance moves. Influence is, without doubt, the Holy Grail of selling – the ability to persuade someone to make a purchase, see the value in your product or service, and believe that what you're offering is exactly what they need. It's a skill that all salespeople strive for but few truly master.

From the seller's perspective, influence is everything. It's the difference between completing a transaction and losing a potential buyer forever. In today's market, where consumers have more options than ever before, influencing a buyer's decision can mean the difference between success and failure.

So, what exactly is influence?

At its core, influence is the ability to guide someone towards a particular decision or action. It's about understanding your buyer's needs, wants, and desires, and using that knowledge to create a connection and establish trust. Traditionally, you would say that the keys to successful influence would be listening, building rapport, and then adapting your product or service to match what your buyer has said. You need to be able to articulate the benefits of what you're selling in a way that resonates with your buyer. You need to be able to answer their questions and address any concerns they may have.

The problem is, of course, as we have discussed before, more than 85% of the buying is done without the seller, and the trend is for that to increase, with the majority of people not wanting a seller involved at all. Again, I will acknowledge that this trend differs between the type of sale you are doing, but the value of the deal that people are comfortable doing without a seller is only increasing, and it's increasing exponentially.

So, who can influence the buyer? Well, that comes down to who is writing the content the buyer is consuming as they research. Whether this is your website, social media post, brochures, or ads, 80% of the influence is no longer handled by part of the organization that has often been in competition with sellers – marketing.

As this is exactly why we need to move the dial. It is why we advocate the thinking of one department and not two. It's why joint goals and rewards are so important. We can no longer do things the way we used to. We can't continue doing what is comfortable because that is how it is done.

It reminds me of the story of how the USA developed their train gauge (as a true nerd, I really like trains!). BTW, so that you know, a train gauge is the distance between the rails. The US standard railroad gauge is 4 feet, 8.5 inches. Odd number, but so what?

Why was that gauge used? Well, because that's the way they built them here in England, and our engineers designed the first US railroads. But why did we build them like that? Because the first rail lines were built by the same people who built the wagon tramways, and that's the gauge they used.

So, why did 'they' use that gauge? Because the people who built the tramways used the same jigs and tools they had used for building wagons, which used that same wheel spacing.

Why did the wagons have that particularly odd wheel spacing? Because if they tried to use any other spacing, the wagon wheels would break more often on some of the old, long-distance roads, as that's the spacing of the wheel ruts.

So, who built those old, rutted roads? Imperial Rome built the first long-distance roads in Europe for their legions. Those roads have been used ever since, and it was the Roman war chariots that formed the initial ruts, which everyone else had to match or risk destroying their wagon wheels. Since the chariots were made for Imperial Rome, they were alike regarding wheel spacing.

And this space was derived by the width of two horses' backsides! Therefore, the United States standard railroad gauge of 4 feet, 8.5 inches is derived from the original specifications for an Imperial Roman war chariot, or the width of two horses' rear ends. Modern, huh!?

It gets worse. You will remember the Space Shuttle? It consisted of the plane part (the shuttle itself) and a huge fuel tank, and then two solid rocket boosters or SRBs. These SRBs are made by a company called Thiokol, at their factory in Utah, and the engineers who designed the SRBs would have preferred to make them a bit fatter. However, the SRBs had to be shipped by train from the factory to the launch site.

Yep, you guessed it, a major Space Shuttle design feature, of what was the world's most advanced transportation system, was determined over 2,000 years ago by the width of a horse's bottom.

And this is the same with selling. How we work in silos for sales and marketing was designed for a different age – a time when the seller had more control and more influence early in the selling process.

As I've mentioned a few times already, I don't want you to think that marketing is more important than sellers or that sellers have no place. That is exactly the thinking I want to break down. Whether you are in selling or in marketing, we are in the business of revenue. When we combine working together with one clear goal, one set of leadership, and joint rewards, the results jump off the page.

If influence is the product of awareness and resonance, it doesn't take Einstein to work out that the skills of marketers and sellers must combine. Marketers are traditionally brilliant at awareness. Sellers are traditionally brilliant at resonance.

I know this is difficult for some, those who have built empires on previous thinking, but it's time to rethink and remember that what got us here is unlikely to get us there.

We need a change in thinking, attitude, and ego.

Let's stop pretending to be one department (I am looking at you CROs who still have a marketing leader and sales leader reporting to them). We need to come together to create a new vision for a revenue organization that is devoid of the previous ways of thinking – something that is fit for today's buyers (and not based on two horses' rears!).

Chapter 4

How big is your pie?

Scarcity or abundance

I am going to get a little theoretical at the beginning of this chapter before moving to a more philosophical position, and I must admit to being somewhat nervous about penning my thoughts here, as this chapter has the potential to be the most contentious of all because we will be discussing some very deeply engrained behaviours that are prevalent across revenue-generating departments.

Have you ever wondered why some people always seem to just be successful in whatever they do, while others seem to struggle with everything? There are arguments to suggest that some individuals are gifted or have some form of privilege, and all of this is true; however, there is another factor. In fact, there is nothing really secret here at all; it is simply based on one factor that influences our experiences and outcomes: our mindset. Specifically, it is whether we embrace a mindset of scarcity or abundance.

Understanding the scarcity mindset

The scarcity mindset is rooted in the belief that resources, opportunities, and possibilities are limited.

Research (Mullainathan, 2013) shows us that individuals with this mindset tend to view the world through a lens of lack and deprivation. They constantly worry about not having enough, and they fear that they will miss out on essential things.

This mindset can lead to feelings of anxiety, competition, and a general sense of scarcity in various aspects of life. Note the link there with competition and anxiety, and our discussions in Chapter 2 around mental fitness.

A scarcity mindset often manifests in negative thought patterns, such as: 'There's not enough time', 'I'll never be successful', or 'There's only one winner, and it won't be me'. These beliefs limit individuals' ability to think creatively, take risks, and seize opportunities. Consequently, the scarcity mindset becomes a self-fulfilling prophecy, perpetuating a cycle of lack and missed potential. Sound familiar?

Embracing the abundance mindset

In contrast, the abundance mindset is based on the belief that opportunities, resources, and possibilities are plentiful. Research (Dweck, 2006) shows us that those with an abundance mindset approach life with optimism, gratitude, and a sense of possibility. They believe that there is enough to go around, and that success is not a zero-sum game (take note of this later in this chapter when we discuss competition and negotiation).

Individuals with an abundance mindset view challenges as opportunities for growth and learning. They are more likely to take risks, seek collaboration, and cultivate a positive attitude. This mindset fuels creativity, resilience, and a willingness to explore new avenues, leading to increased well-being and success.

Shifting from scarcity to abundance

The good news is that our mindset is not fixed; it can be transformed. It's difficult, especially after years of thinking one way, but it can be done.

Here are a few strategies to help make the shift (I have added the research in for those that are sceptical, as I know this is an area where people often think mindset is more of a nice idea rather than something based in science):

- **Cultivate gratitude:** Practising gratitude is a powerful tool for cultivating an abundance mindset. By focusing on what we have instead of what we lack, we begin to appreciate the abundance already present in our lives (Emmons, 2003).

- **Reframe limiting beliefs:** Challenge and reframe negative, scarcity-based beliefs. Replace thoughts like 'I can't' with 'I can find a way' or 'I have the ability to learn and grow' (Seligman, 2018).

- **Practise abundance mentality:** Actively seek out opportunities for collaboration, sharing, and supporting others. The belief in abundance fosters an environment of cooperation and abundance for all (Covey, 2004).

While not all of them directly examine these mindsets, they contribute to our understanding of the underlying beliefs, attitudes, and behaviours associated with scarcity and abundance orientations. By considering the findings and recommendations from these studies, we can begin to shift our mindset and embrace a more abundant perspective.

But what stops people from making this move? Why do people continue to harbour and develop a mindset that is shaped by scarcity?

A few factors are at play here – but first, let me address one issue. The scarcity/abundance mindset has limitations, as we need to consider those who have literally nothing. It's quite difficult to think abundantly about a resource like water when you live in a desert or an area lacking infrastructure. An abundance mindset, while powerful, cannot conjure something from nothing. It may be true that having nothing drives a person to resolve the issue, but to believe that simply thinking abundantly makes it happen is misguided, regardless of how well-meaning it may be.

The two biggest saboteurs that prevent people from moving their mindsets are old-fashioned pride and self-protection.

For me, pride is the single most destructive force we humans possess. It drives us to do unthinkable things to other things and other people and is the root cause of every war, every argument, and every destructive element of our lives. I know this is strong, but challenge me on it. Everything falls back to pride. In our mindset, we don't want to be wrong; we don't want to move from our current position, as it has probably served us well.

To admit their way of thinking was wrong is just too much – too much to give up, too much to have to change. I am aware my view might be too 'Pollyanna', but I am convinced that if we were to deal with pride as the root cause of the issues of this world, the world would be a much better place.

The second, and I have already touched on it briefly, concerns self-protection.

There is an old saying that any strength, when overdone, becomes a weakness, and this holds true in this context. For many individuals, adopting a scarcity mindset has proven beneficial. It has safeguarded them from overspending, driven their competitiveness for promotions over colleagues, and assisted them in achieving number one status – you can see where I'm heading. However, the issue is that while all of this may be valid, when taken to extremes, the repercussions, as previously discussed, can be tremendously damaging.

The problem is, to be able to see the damage, you need to think bigger and wider than just you, and thus we revolve back to pride.

Breaking bad

For all this good stuff on mindset to really have an impact, we need to break what we thought we knew. Just like the story of the width of train tracks in the last chapter, we are still too defined by what has happened before and not focused enough on thinking through what we need now.

However, much like the train track story, there is a cost involved. Replacing the train tracks with alternatives that better suit today's needs would be expensive, and many would argue that it is prohibitively so. Yet, if we are not brave enough to change and invest in new approaches, we will remain trapped – making compromises indefinitely and miss out on the benefits of new models.

Many reasons for the difficulty in changing stem from the insidious nature of today's obsession with short-term results. Our drive to fulfil five-year plans to exit, or the constant pressure to meet ever-increasing targets every 92 days, often prevents us from stepping back to consider the longer term and genuinely invest in the future, even if it proves challenging at first.

However, rough seas make strong sailors, and if we can detach ourselves from our own pride, which believes we are more important than the next generation or the next set of owners, the long-term outlook is bleaker than we realize as we lurch from one short-term plan to another.

Fun or folly

More than probably any other work setting, selling has a culture of competitiveness. This has been a foundation and central tenet of every single sales organization and sales leader I have ever met. It has bred a culture where getting to the top is the ultimate goal. Being seen to be on the leaderboard or getting entry to the President's Club for top performers is seen as the ultimate accolade.

The deep-rooted behaviour is enjoyed by the types of people you would expect, and I know I am stereotyping here. Still, these tend to be the Type-A personalities (characterized by a competitive and ambitious nature, a strong drive for achievement, a sense of urgency, and a tendency towards high stress and impatience levels) normally associated with successful sellers.

I have met and sparred with many sales leaders who believe that sales competition is vital. I have even had some sales leaders say that without a leaderboard and a culture of competitiveness, their sales would not exist, and they would not hire a seller without a competitive nature. Unsurprisingly, they were quite aggressive about it, and 'quite' is an understatement.

But does it actually work?

I have absolutely no doubt that it works in the short term, as I have seen it first-hand. However, you should know by now, by reading this far, that I am not interested in short-term solutions.

I also do not doubt that it *can* be beneficial. When executed well, adding some spice can be good. But as I said earlier, any strength overdone is a weakness. Ultimately, I do not belong to the camp that believes everyone should receive a participant's medal merely for showing up. Excellent performance should be rewarded, and some will perform better than others. There is certainly such a thing as 1st, 2nd, and 3rd… and even last!

What I am advocating for is the distinction between healthy and unhealthy competition, and ensuring that our default stance does not lean towards the toxicity of an unhealthy highly competitive culture.

So, what is the difference between healthy and unhealthy competition?

Healthy competition is a positive and constructive form of competition in which individuals or teams strive to improve their performance, skills, and abilities. It involves a fair and ethical pursuit of goals while maintaining respect for others. Healthy competition is characterized by collaboration, learning, personal growth, and a supportive work environment.

On the other hand, unhealthy competition refers to a negative and detrimental form of competition that undermines individuals, teams, or the overall work environment. It involves behaviours that prioritize personal gain over the well-being of others, including sabotage, hostility, unethical practices, and a focus on short-term wins at the expense of long-term success. Unhealthy competition often leads to a toxic work environment, reduced morale, stress, and negative impacts on individuals' well-being.

The problem here is that many people could read these differently. For example, many people who I would say operate a toxic culture would not believe what they are doing undermines individuals or teams but binds them together. I would be able to convincingly argue the opposite.

To resolve this, let's go a little deeper into the research and explore a few more differences. Here are some key distinctions that, again, might help you decide which side of the fence you sit on. I've added a source for each statement should you wish to go even deeper (there is a whole other book on this topic).

Collaboration vs. undermining

Healthy competition promotes collaboration and cooperation among employees, where they support and learn from each other. The unhealthy competition involves undermining or sabotaging colleagues to gain a personal advantage (Harvard, 2024).

I see a lot of this in many competitive workplaces. The drive to be number 1, rather than bringing people together, creates division and, in extreme (but not uncommon) cases, people actually trying to take down a colleague. Even worse, we can see this when marketing and sales play off each other. Marketing blames sales for not closing more. Sales blames marketing for not providing quality leads.

Any competition should be focused not on the individual but on the team. Rewarding a single person over everyone else will simply drive the wrong behaviour. While the individual prospers, the rest of the organization is damaged.

Personal growth vs. self-destruction

Healthy competition focuses on personal growth and development, encouraging individuals to improve their skills and knowledge. Unhealthy competition can lead to self-destruction as individuals prioritize winning over their own well-being and may engage in unethical behaviour (Today, 2024). Again, I've seen this too many times. The requirement to work every hour, or to be seen as the most productive, in the vain hope you will be recognized above your co-workers.

It would be easy to say that this is an individual's own issue, and it is. Still, it is something that should not even be a conversation and only exists because workplaces are fostering a working environment that encourages the 'more is better' approach.

Supportive culture vs. toxic culture

Healthy competition is supported by a positive organizational culture, recognizing achievements, providing fair evaluation systems, and encouraging collaboration. Unhealthy competition creates a toxic culture with fear, mistrust, and hostility, leading to stress and decreased job satisfaction (Forbes, 2015).

When it's put as clearly as this, I am still stunned to be arguing with people who genuinely believe that high-stress competition is the right way. They are effectively saying, 'Yes, I accept that there will be fear, mistrust, and hostility, but that's the only way we hit our number' – like hitting your number is the *only* important thing. If you think like that, I am afraid you have missed the point.

Don't get me wrong; we all have numbers to hit, but creating a toxic culture is not the only way to achieve them. It shows a lack of imagination, innovation, and humanity.

Constructive feedback vs. criticism

Healthy competition fosters constructive feedback and learning from both successes and failures. Unhealthy competition involves constant criticism and negativity, hindering personal and professional growth (*Journal of Business and Industrial Marketing*, 2020).

One of the most successful environments I have witnessed was an organization with a no-blame culture. Now, they were not all sitting around on cushions chanting; these were highly skilled professionals with hard numbers to hit and difficult jobs to do. But when something went wrong, they didn't look to the person and find blame; they looked to the systems that caused it to fail.

Very few people get up in the morning intending to set the world on fire and, very often, it is a system somewhere that has failed rather than a person doing something wrong.

Did people still get fired? Sure they did, but it was more about helping that person find a better fit for themselves than degrading them and telling them they are rubbish.

Employee turnover is more a representation of management than it is the organization. There is a popular statistic that backs this up. According to a Gallup study (2017), approximately 50% of employees surveyed reported having left a job at some point in their career to get away from their manager. The study emphasized the critical role of managers in employee engagement and retention. So that's 1 in 2!

Ask most managers why people leave, and you will get the answer that they wanted more money or wanted to be developed. Really?

Team cohesion vs. division

Healthy competition enhances team cohesion as individuals collaborate towards common goals, share ideas, and support one another. Unhealthy competition can result in divisions and conflicts within teams, with individuals prioritizing their own success over collective achievement (*Journal of Psychology*, 2013).

And again, where competition leads to separation and division, we will find an unhealthy culture.

I won't labour the point here any further, only to ask you to be curious about you and your company's performance metrics, especially ones where there is a competitive element. Are they healthy or unhealthy? Do your goals bring you and your company together, or do they create division? Be curious. Challenge the thinking.

But what about our competition – the people and organizations that are also trying to win our business?

Fight, flight, or fright

Anyone with even the slightest education in business studies knows that competition is a good thing. However, I am not going to assume everyone has had the benefit, so please indulge me as I go into teacher mode: healthy competition in a healthy market is good for many reasons. Let's look at a few of them.

Innovation and progress

Competition encourages businesses to innovate and improve their products, services, and operations to gain a competitive edge. The drive to outperform rivals leads to developing new technologies, processes, and ideas, ultimately benefiting consumers and society. It fosters a culture of continuous improvement and pushes businesses to strive for excellence.

Consumer benefits

When businesses compete, consumers tend to benefit from better quality products, lower prices, increased choices, and improved customer service. Companies are motivated to offer superior value to attract and retain buyers, leading to more affordable and accessible options in the market. Competition empowers consumers with greater purchasing power and the ability to make informed decisions.

Economic growth

Competition stimulates economic growth by encouraging productivity, efficiency, and investment. Businesses strive to optimize their operations to remain competitive, which often results in increased productivity and the efficient allocation of resources. Pursuing market share and profitability drives companies to expand, hire more employees, and invest in research and development, contributing to economic development and job creation.

Entrepreneurship and creativity

Competition encourages entrepreneurship and the formation of new businesses. It creates an environment where individuals with innovative ideas and solutions can enter the market and compete with established players. The prospect of success and the potential rewards incentivize entrepreneurial activity, leading to the discovery of new markets, products, and business models. This promotes a dynamic and vibrant economy.

Accountability and ethical conduct

In a competitive market, businesses are held accountable for their actions. They must maintain high ethical standards, provide value to buyers, and operate transparently to retain their competitive position. Competing firms keep each other in check, as competitors can expose and exploit any unethical behaviour or poor business practices. This fosters a culture of integrity and responsible business conduct.

However, it's worth noting that while healthy competition can bring numerous benefits, it also has potential downsides. For balance, let's look at the negative consequences of unhealthy competition.

Monopolies and market dominance

Unhealthy competition can lead to the consolidation of power and the emergence of monopolies or dominant players in the market. When a single company gains excessive control over an industry, it can manipulate prices, reduce consumer choices, and stifle innovation. This can result in decreased competition, reduced efficiency, and new business entry barriers.

Price wars and predatory practices

Unhealthy competition may trigger price wars, where businesses use aggressive price-cutting strategies to gain market share. While this may initially benefit consumers with lower prices, it can become unsustainable and lead to business financial losses. Smaller companies may struggle to compete with larger competitors and may be forced out of the market. Predatory practices, such as dumping products below cost to drive competitors out of business, can harm the market's overall health.

Reduced quality and innovation

Unhealthy competition can incentivize businesses to prioritize short-term gains over long-term investments in quality and innovation. Companies may cut corners, compromise product or service quality, or neglect research and development efforts in a race to reduce costs and maximize profits. This can result in inferior products, diminished experiences, and a lack of innovation in the industry.

Negative externalities

Unhealthy competition can lead to negative externalities, such as environmental degradation or social harm. In a bid to gain a competitive advantage, businesses may disregard sustainable practices, exploit resources, or neglect their social responsibilities. These actions can have adverse effects on the environment, local communities, and society at large.

Employee exploitation

In an intensely competitive environment, businesses may pressure employees to work longer hours, accept lower wages, or tolerate poor working conditions. The focus on cost-cutting and maximizing profits can lead to employee exploitation and a disregard for their well-being. This can result in high turnover rates, low job satisfaction, and decreased overall employee welfare.

In summary, healthy competition is good; unhealthy competition is bad.

I am sure we have all participated in or been invited to sales training sessions where we have been encouraged to destroy, outsmart, outshine, or out manoeuvre the competition. The revenue industry has conditioned us to view competition as a negative aspect, something we must defeat at every opportunity.

There are training courses and books that teach us ways, techniques, and methods to unsettle the buyer so they are persuaded to buy our product, rather than the competition's – even if it is superior and a better fit.

I have even attended training sessions (thankfully, not one I planned or designed) where the sales leaders arrived in military fatigues, drawing the analogy of us being at war and shouting: 'Show us your game face.' For the movie buffs out there, this was directly from *Full Metal Jacket*, and we all know how that line of thinking ended, which serves as another direct reference to why mental fitness is so important.

In one legendary session that I have been told of, the business leader actually turned up in a tank! A full-on, real TANK.

Now, the awful, outdated, and frankly pathetic macho messaging aside, why are our revenue generators being taught that competition is bad when it is, in fact, the reverse: that competition is healthy and should be welcomed? Why do we want our business to become the very vision of unhealthy competition?

When you stop and think about it, it's simply bizarre.

Our language reflects this notion, as we either *win* a deal from a competitor or *lose* a deal to one. The phrasing implies that there are only two options – and neither involves the buyer!

For me, the vision of healthy competition is perfect. Our role in this is to ensure our products are the best they can be to add value to the buyer based on the merits and benefits of the product.

Achieving this demands excellent product management, effective pricing strategies, robust marketing, proficient selling, and strong customer success. This is why Infinite exists. If a buyer opts for a product other than ours, we should be thankful as it indicates either that the buyer was not qualified in the first place or that our competitors' products are superior, which should motivate us to improve. And when we improve, everyone benefits.

This all goes back to the abundance and scarcity mentality. Those with a scarcity mentality will see every lost deal as someone stealing from their pie. However, people with an abundance mentality realize it was not their pie in the first place, *and* there is not just one pie, but an unlimited supply of pies.

Competition should not be feared, and it should not be destroyed. It should be welcomed and respected. In practice, this means we need to be comfortable to:

- walk away when the competition has beaten you on the product merits, rather than trying to outsmart them;
- co-exist where it makes sense;
- acknowledge the competition for what it brings to us all; and
- never (and I mean *never*) disrespect the competition, either in front of the buyer or inside the business.

This last point is something I struggle with. I am good in front of a buyer, but not so much when I am with my colleagues. It's a personal area of growth, but I know it's important as it's an unhealthy attitude that drives the wrong behaviours, and I know my attitude rubs off on others, so the effect is compounded.

None of us are perfect. We can stop this negativity when we change our behaviours. If we can really embrace the goodness of healthy competition and drop the embarrassingly childish anti-competition behaviours, there is a whole world out there for us to explore and benefit from.

If the buyer chooses our competitor's product or service over ours, there is only one reason. We (product, person, price, or company) didn't fit. Don't hate someone else for it. Learn from it.

I am also not naïve enough to know that others won't take advantage of us if we play nice. They will. And that's fine. Let them play a different game rather than continuing to push the roundabout.

Like most of what we are trying to position in this book and methodology, the old ways are broken, and the only way to replace them is to be brave enough to stop so we can get the reset we, our buyers, and our economy need.

And this isn't just in how we deal with our competitors, but should also be in how we deal with our buyers as we go into negotiations.

More pie, Vicar?

Negotiation (this can be a vast subject, deserving of its own book), much like competition and competitiveness, is often shrouded in negative and aggressive language. It is seen as something we either win or lose. Being a good negotiator frequently translates to being harsh, brutal, or hard. We are praised, if not sometimes worshipped, if we can negotiate well. It's where the big kids play.

Negotiation theory has, thankfully, changed a lot, and it is much more focused on win–win, partially thanks to the popularity of the work from the likes of the educator, author, and businessman Stephen Covey.

If you have not come across this term before, a win–win strategy, also known as a collaborative or integrative strategy, is an approach to problem-solving and negotiation where all parties involved aim to achieve mutually beneficial outcomes.

It emphasizes cooperation, open communication, and finding solutions that satisfy the interests and needs of all stakeholders. In a win–win strategy, success is not measured by one party's gain at the expense of others, but rather by the creation of value for everyone involved.

A win–win strategy acknowledges that the success of one party does not have to come at the expense of others. It promotes a cooperative mindset, seeks innovative solutions, and builds relationships based on trust and mutual respect. A win–win strategy sets the stage for sustainable and positive outcomes by focusing on shared interests and creating value.

This is why I employed the pie analogy for this chapter. Rather than fixating on winning or losing, and the stringent, absolute boundaries that creates, we should concentrate on expanding the pie or seeking out additional pies. The falsehood is that there is only one pie.

Our enemy is not the people we are negotiating with. Our mindset and beliefs will betray us, and we need to work hard on shifting our focus.

You see, win–lose, lose–win, or lose–lose negotiations often result in strained relationships and heightened conflict. In contrast, win–win negotiations aim to preserve and strengthen relationships by considering the interests of all parties involved. By focusing on collaborative problem-solving and open communication, win–win negotiations reduce the likelihood of resentment, animosity, and future disputes.

This can save time, resources, and emotional energy that would otherwise be spent on resolving conflicts.

I find it astonishing that anyone can believe that any deal being made that has the word 'lose' on either side of the equation is a good deal. If we, as sellers, win over our buyers, but they have somehow lost, we have done them a terrible disservice merely to line our pockets. Similarly, if the buyer wins over us as sellers, they are shooting themselves in the foot.

And don't even get me started on those who believe in lose–lose. I know a few of these types, and they would genuinely prefer an option where both parties lose if they cannot win. Talk about limiting and destructive beliefs.

A win–win attitude demands much from us. It requires significant mental fitness as well as the courage to think differently. Most importantly, it necessitates that we think bigger – bigger in terms of the scope of the deal and the timeline.

As I said with competition, will having a win–win mindset put us at a disadvantage and mean some will get one over on us? It will always be possible, as many people (buyers and sellers) continue to hold different values, and that's perfectly acceptable. Contrary to what you might be taught, you don't have to win everything. If anyone experiences a win–lose, lose–win, or lose–lose scenario, you can be certain that this will only be the case in the short term.

Don't stress it. Doff your cap and move on to another pie, accompanied by a humble side of lessons learned along the way.

Like investing in huge infrastructure projects, you might not be around to see the benefits yourself, as you might have moved on, but it was for the greater good. And this is why we also need to ensure we have the right incentives.

Carrots, sticks, and cabbages

Commissions, bonuses, incentives, rewards – whatever you call them – they're one of those things no one really wants to question too closely.

When you think of salespeople, you imagine sellers driving flashy cars in shiny suits and carrying expensive briefcases. Thankfully, while the briefcases and shiny suits may have faded (cars still seem to be popular, mind you, and briefcases are enjoying a minor renaissance), the driving force behind them hasn't changed. Have you ever considered what drives the behaviour of these sellers and whether much of what's been mentioned before has been shaped in the past by inappropriate sales incentives?

Sales incentives have been around since the very beginning of sales and are based on the simple theory that the more you sell, the more money you make.

The more we can extract money from our buyers, the more we can give to our sellers. And because everything is so measurable and there is such a direct connection between what is being sold and money in the bank, it is easy to align.

Sales incentives come in different flavours and are based on basic incentive theory. The following theories aim to understand what drives performance and how incentives can effectively enhance productivity and achieve organizational goals. Here are a few well-known incentive theories for sellers.

- **Goal setting theory:** This theory suggests that setting specific, challenging goals can motivate individuals to perform better. In the sales context, sellers are provided with targets or quotas to achieve, and incentives are tied to their goal attainment. The theory emphasizes that goals should be realistic, measurable, and time-bound to drive motivation. This is popularized by the acronym SMART (Specific (or sometimes Sustainable), Measurable, Achievable, Realistic, and Time-bound).

- **Expectancy theory:** According to this theory, individuals are motivated to exert effort when they believe their efforts will lead to desirable outcomes. Sellers are motivated by the expectation that their sales performance will result in rewards, such as monetary bonuses, commissions, recognition, or career advancement. The theory emphasizes the importance of perceived effort-to-performance expectancy and performance-to-reward expectancy.

- **Equity theory:** This theory suggests that individuals strive for fairness and equity in their relationships. In the context of sales incentives, sellers compare their inputs (e.g., effort, time, skills) and outputs (e.g., rewards, recognition) to those of their peers or industry standards. If they perceive an inequity, such as receiving lower rewards than their colleagues despite similar efforts, it can lead to demotivation. Therefore, ensuring that incentive structures are perceived as fair and equitable is important.

- **Reinforcement theory:** This theory focuses on the relationship between behaviour and its consequences. It suggests that sales-people can be motivated through positive reinforcement, such as providing rewards or recognition for meeting or exceeding sales targets. By linking rewards directly to desired sales behaviours, sellers are encouraged to repeat those behaviours in the future.
- **Social cognitive theory:** This theory emphasizes the role of observational learning and self-efficacy in motivation. Sellers can be motivated by observing and modelling the behaviour of successful peers or role models. Additionally, enhancing their self-efficacy, or belief in their own capabilities, through training, coaching, and feedback, can positively influence their motivation and performance.

It's important to note that organizations may employ various combinations of these theories or adapt them to their specific contexts and selling organizations. The effectiveness of incentive theories can vary based on factors such as industry, organizational culture, individual differences, and market conditions.

And they work. There is very strong evidence and correlation that sales incentives can change the performance of an individual or team. When designed and implemented properly, sales incentives can provide several benefits.

- **Motivation and goal alignment:** Incentives can align sales-people's goals with the organization's objectives. By linking rewards to desired sales behaviours, such as meeting sales targets, acquiring new buyers, or increasing revenue, incentives can motivate sales teams to put in their best efforts to achieve these goals.
- **Performance improvement:** Well-designed incentives can boost performance by providing a tangible reward for achieving

or exceeding targets. Incentives create a sense of urgency and drive sellers to go the extra mile, resulting in increased productivity and revenue generation.

- **Focus and prioritization:** Incentives help sales teams to prioritize their efforts and focus on activities that directly contribute to sales success. By tying incentives to specific metrics or behaviours, organizations can influence sellers' behaviour and guide them towards the most important sales objectives.

- **Retention and engagement:** Incentives can enhance employee engagement and satisfaction. Salespeople who are rewarded for their efforts and see a clear link between performance and rewards are likelier to feel valued and remain motivated. In turn, this can contribute to higher employee retention rates and reduce turnover in the sales force.

- **Competition and collaboration:** Well-structured incentives can foster healthy competition among sales team members, driving them to excel and outperform their peers. Additionally, incentives can encourage collaboration by rewarding teamwork, knowledge sharing, and support among sales team members, leading to a more cohesive and effective sales force.

But you need to be careful what you wish for, as the more perceptive of you can probably already see that, while these incentives work, there is a dark side. Let's look at a couple of stories about where sales incentives went wrong and backfired:

Wells Fargo account scandal

The Wells Fargo account scandal unfolded in 2016 and remains one of the most notable cases in recent history where sales incentives led to severe negative consequences. The scandal exposed the unethical practices that took place within Wells Fargo Bank, one of the largest banks in the USA.

Wells Fargo's aggressive sales culture and incentive programmes were at the heart of the scandal. The bank had established ambitious sales goals for its employees, encouraging them to cross-sell various financial products to buyers. These goals were tied to performance evaluations, promotions, and significant financial incentives for employees who met or exceeded their targets.

Sounds pretty normal, right? Nothing to see here. It's what every organization does, isn't it? But let's look at what happened.

To meet these demanding goals, employees resorted to fraudulent tactics. They opened unauthorized bank and credit card accounts, transferred funds without consent, and manipulated data. These unauthorized accounts were created to artificially inflate sales numbers, meet targets, and earn incentives.

The scandal came to light when internal whistle-blowers and investigative journalists exposed the fraudulent practices within the bank. The public outrage was immediate and widespread. Wells Fargo faced significant backlash from regulators, lawmakers, and customers, leading to a tarnished reputation and a substantial decline in stock value.

The consequences for Wells Fargo were severe. Regulatory authorities fined the bank billions of dollars for its improper practices. Top executives, including the CEO, were forced to resign, and thousands of employees were terminated. The scandal resulted in a loss of trust and confidence from customers, shareholders, and the general public – the latter of which is still going on with a huge mistrust of the banking sector dominating public opinion.

While this scandal is a cautionary tale about the potential dangers of aggressive sales cultures and misaligned incentives, it also highlights the importance of maintaining ethical standards and fostering a culture that prioritizes customer well-being and trust.

Volkswagen emissions scandal

This story is less about individual sellers but rather an organization's need to take market share (see my earlier comments on competition).

The Volkswagen emissions scandal, also known as 'Dieselgate', unfolded in 2015 and exposed one of the largest automotive industry scandals in recent memory. The scandal centred around Volkswagen's deliberate manipulation of emissions tests for its diesel vehicles, leading to severe environmental and legal repercussions. In an effort to meet strict emission standards imposed by regulatory bodies, Volkswagen installed sophisticated software known as 'defeat devices' in their diesel cars. These devices could detect when a vehicle was undergoing emissions testing and adjust the engine performance to meet regulatory requirements. However, during real-world driving conditions, the vehicles emitted significantly higher levels of harmful pollutants, such as nitrogen oxide (NOx), than allowed.

The scandal came to light when independent researchers and the International Council on Clean Transportation discovered discrepancies between emissions levels in Volkswagen vehicles during laboratory testing and on-road driving. The revelation sent shockwaves throughout the automotive industry and ignited a global outcry. The consequences for Volkswagen were extensive and far-reaching. The company faced legal actions, lawsuits, and significant financial penalties. It had to recall millions of vehicles worldwide, leading to massive costs and damage to its brand reputation. The scandal also led to a decline in sales and a loss of consumer trust.

While it is challenging to provide an exact figure due to ongoing legal proceedings and various associated expenses, the scandal has had significant financial implications for the company. As at time of writing, Volkswagen estimated that the scandal had cost the company over €32 billion (US$35 billion) in fines, settlements, legal fees, vehicle recalls, and other related expenses.

€32 billion – was it worth it?

For me, the Volkswagen emissions scandal was not just a financial and PR disaster. It also managed to expose the ethical implications of prioritizing sales and market share over responsibility, and firmly backs up my position that in generating revenue, we hold the keys to much more than just our products but in many cases are responsible for a much broader remit and should be held accountable.

We need joined-up thinking and incentives that support it – and that means being brave enough to rethink the models we've treated as untouchable for too long.

What I am about to say is going to be hugely unpopular with most of the people reading this, but I ask you to remain open-minded on this and, again, think beyond the immediate future. I am sure if you have got this far and have not burned this book as heresy already, you are already in that mindset, but sit down for this one.

The days of sales commission need to stop.

OK, I said that for dramatic effect as I don't believe *all* sales commission needs to stop, but I do believe that 'seller *only*' commission needs to stop.

If we truly believe in revenue as the future of selling, then we need to review everything we believe about incentives and make sure they are collaborative. Rather than individual sales targets, accelerators, and the like, we should consider one of the following models.

- **Team-based incentives:** In our concept of revenue teams, which include both sales and marketing functions, incentives should focus on collective performance and revenue generation. The team as a whole should be incentivized based on achieving overall revenue targets or specific business metrics, such as revenue growth or customer acquisition.
- **Cross-functional collaboration:** Incentives for revenue teams can be designed to encourage collaboration and alignment between sales, marketing, and customer success. This can involve shared incentives that reward collaboration,

joint planning, and successful lead handoffs between the two teams.

- **Customer satisfaction and retention:** In addition to revenue generation, incentives for revenue teams may also consider customer satisfaction and retention metrics. This encourages the team to focus on acquiring new customers and providing excellent customer experiences to drive repeat business and long-term customer relationships.

- **Balanced metrics:** Incentives for revenue teams could include a combination of leading and lagging indicators. Leading indicators could include activities like lead generation, pipeline development, or marketing campaign success. Lagging indicators include revenue, new customer acquisition, and lifetime value. This balanced approach ensures that both short-term sales targets and long-term growth are considered.

As you can see, there are many more creative ways to provide incentives – ones that can generate the right behaviours and motivate the whole team, levelling what is currently a very skewed approach. Overall, this team-based incentive approach should promote collaboration and cooperation among revenue team members, leading to improved performance. When team members are motivated by a shared reward, they are more likely to work together, share knowledge, and support each other.

This approach can also leverage team members' diverse skills and expertise (remember what we said about cognitive diversity). By pooling their talents, teams can solve complex problems more effectively and achieve better outcomes. And, most importantly, team-focused incentives can foster a sense of shared purpose and align individual goals with team objectives, leading to increased commitment and effort from team members.

It's rare for turkeys to vote for Christmas and rarer for sellers to think outside of their own pocket, but when you look at the clear benefits, it should become a no-brainer to revise how we incentivize. Let's not be naïve, though, like our attitude towards competitiveness, competition, and negotiation; it will only come when we realize there is more than one pie and that when one person is rewarded, it doesn't mean there is less for you.

Will we miss out on some talent that only wants huge incentives? Yep. But are these the sorts of sellers we want to be working with? If their overriding attitude is self-focused, do we really want them to be the primary relationship with our buyers?

I am very aware that this whole chapter will bring out many emotions. Some will think I am a little idealistic, some will think the approach is good but naïve, and some will just downright hate it. I know this, as I have had plenty of heated arguments with many sellers and leaders with opposing views.

So, if we have all these pies, where can we find the cutlery to eat them with? This is when you need to get your map out!

Part 2

The INFINITE methodology

Chapter 5

A map, not a process

Maps vs. routes

One of the main reasons Matt and I decided to write this book was the realization that even books on sales written in 2020 or later all look at the way we *used* to sell. Sure, there are some updates from older methodologies, but they seem to be an additive to an older way of thinking.

This is fine, to an extent, but we wanted to write an approach that was based on how sales look today. You see, most, if not all, of the current books on sales methodologies begin with the sentence: 'When I was working in Xerox…'. Now, to be 100% clear, there is nothing wrong with that statement. Xerox created what is arguably the most outstanding sales enablement programme ever. I can't even begin to fathom how many billions in revenue those programmes have helped to generate. At the time, it was super exciting and totally relevant. It was also controversial, dynamic, and challenging to the sellers of the time. Of course, their programmes were based on adapting and developing the ideas of people like Napoleon Hill and Dale Carnegie. And these were based on the work of the previous generation. Let's have a quick history lesson on where sales methodologies came from.

The history of sales methodologies dates back centuries, evolving alongside the development of commerce and the growth of selling as a profession. From the early days of bartering to the complex sales strategies of today, sales methodologies have played a crucial role in guiding salespeople and organizations to achieve success.

One of the earliest recorded sales methodologies can be traced back to ancient civilizations. In ancient Greece, for example, persuasive techniques were taught to orators, who used their skills to convince people to take specific actions or make purchases. These techniques laid the foundation for the art of persuasion, which has remained a fundamental aspect of selling throughout history.

During the Industrial Revolution in the 18th and 19th centuries, mass production and the rise of large-scale manufacturing created a need for more structured sales approaches. One of the notable methodologies from this era is the AIDA model, which stands for Attention, Interest, Desire, and Action.

This model, introduced in the late 19th century (and still taught to this day), focused on capturing the attention of potential buyers, generating interest in a product or service, building desire, and ultimately motivating them to take action.

In the early 20th century, the concept of consultative selling emerged (and you thought it was a new concept, right?).

This approach emphasized building relationships, understanding their needs, and providing tailored solutions. The idea was to move away from a transactional approach and focus on long-term partnerships. This shift in mindset laid the groundwork for modern sales methodologies, prioritizing buyer-centricity and value creation.

In the 1970s, a new sales methodology called SPIN selling was introduced by Neil Rackham. SPIN stands for Situation, Problem, Implication, and Need-payoff. This methodology emphasized the importance of asking probing questions to uncover customer pain points, understanding the implications of those pain points, and presenting solutions that address the customer's needs. SPIN selling became highly influential and is still widely used today, despite it being more than 50 years old.

The late 20th century saw the emergence of more systematic sales methodologies. One of the most well-known is the 'solution selling' methodology, developed by Michael Bosworth in the 1980s. Solution selling focuses on identifying customer problems and offering tailored solutions to address those problems. It emphasized the importance of understanding the customer's business and aligning the sales process with their buying process.

As technology advanced in the late 20th and early 21st centuries, new sales methodologies were developed to adapt to changing buyer behaviour and the digital landscape. The Challenger Sale, introduced by Matthew Dixon and Brent Adamson in 2011, gained significant attention. This methodology proposed that successful sellers challenge the buyers' thinking, present unique insights, and push them out of their comfort zone. It highlighted the importance of being a trusted advisor and teaching buyers something new.

So, there is nothing new under the sun, and I would bet that everyone has experienced a training session that included at least one of these methodologies in the last few years, despite them being many, many years old.

Now, it could be said that they are still being taught because they are still relevant. And that is true. The basis of AIDA (i.e., attention, interest, desire, action), for example, is still super relevant, as human nature largely remains the same, and if you boil most of the most popular methodologies down, you will probably find AIDA underneath.

The same goes with qualification methods. Solutions such as MEDDIC (or MEDDPIC or other variations) are just extensions of BANT (Budget, Authority, Need, and Time) where the extra granularity helps to drive better insight.

There's one more thing that shows up time and again – and it's another area we've been reluctant to question. It's something every seller knows about (although not every seller uses), and it's something that is the backbone of an entire multi-billion-dollar market sector. And that is the 'sales process'. For those of you who are not sellers, here are the basics.

A sales process refers to a systematic series of steps or stages that sellers follow to move a prospect from the initial stage of awareness or lead generation to the final stage of closing a sale. It provides a structured framework for managing and tracking selling activities, ensuring that the selling team can effectively navigate the buyer's journey and maximize the chances of closing deals.

While specific sales processes may vary across industries and organizations, they generally encompass the following key stages.

- **Prospecting:** This is the initial stage where sellers identify potential prospects and gather information about them. It involves lead generation, researching target markets, and qualifying leads to determine if they fit the ideal buyer profile.
- **Qualification:** Once prospects are identified, the qualification stage involves evaluating their needs, budget, authority, and timeline (recognize that!). This helps salespeople to determine if the prospect is a good fit and has the potential to become a paying customer.
- **Needs assessment:** In this stage, the sellers engage with the prospect to understand their pain points, challenges, and goals. By asking probing questions, actively listening, and conducting thorough discovery conversations, the salesperson gains insights into the prospect's requirements and can tailor their approach accordingly.
- **Solution presentation:** Based on the information gathered during the needs assessment stage, the salesperson presents a solution that addresses the prospect's specific needs. This may involve demonstrating the product or service, showcasing its features and benefits, and highlighting how it can solve the prospect's challenges and achieve their desired outcomes.
- **Objection handling:** During the sales process, prospects may raise objections or concerns. The salesperson must address these objections effectively by providing relevant information, addressing any doubts or hesitations, and offering evidence or testimonials that support the value and credibility of the solution.
- **Closing:** The closing stage involves finalizing the sale and securing the prospect's commitment to becoming a buyer. This

may include negotiating pricing and terms, discussing contracts, and guiding the prospect through decision-making to reach a mutually beneficial agreement.

There can be additional steps too, including the following.

- **Follow-up and post-sale relationship:** After the sale is closed, nurturing the relationship with the buyer is essential. This includes delivering the product or service as promised, providing excellent customer service, and seeking feedback to ensure customer satisfaction. Building strong post-sale relationships can lead to repeat business, referrals, and long-term loyalty.
- **Sales analytics and evaluation:** Throughout the sales process, it is important to track and analyse key performance metrics and evaluate the effectiveness of the selling strategy. This data helps to identify areas for improvement, measure selling team performance, and refine the sales process for better results.

Of course, this list covers just the basics. There are many different versions of sales processes, and while they can all boil down, they tend to be quite unique to the organization. They also form the basis of nearly every Customer Relationship Management (CRM) solution. From Salesforce.com to Membrain, they are all based (and need to be, to work properly) on a sales process that guides a seller along their journey. And it has been a huge success. CRM plays a huge part in every successful selling organization and is a wise investment and, when used properly, can transform your revenue by itself.

There is yet another book I could write on this subject, and I don't plan to go into the detail of successful CRM implementation, but I will say this: It is never the CRM's fault if you are not extracting value – it's how you use it that really matters. You may have noticed a few challenges, however.

1) Sales processes are largely seller-focused. In other words, they are based on how we want to sell, not on how the buyer wants to buy. There has been progress in this area in recent years, moving towards a buyer-centric sales process, but in many cases, it is just a sales process renamed.

2) It implies a linear progression. A sales process has a start, an end, and stops in between. You move between steps after certain work has been done or the buyer completes a certain action.

3) It treats everyone the same. Everyone goes through the same process, whether you are a CEO or an office manager. It's true that more sophisticated companies have either different sales processes for their target markets or have contextualized each step depending on whom they are selling to, but everyone takes the same route.

And again, I am not knocking this, as it works. The size of the CRM market is a testament to that alone. The problem is not that it doesn't work. It's simply that there is a better way – something more adaptable to meet the needs of the buyers, and something that can flex to appeal to even more people. This is because people are different. Let me give you a silly example from my personal life.

If my dad and I were driving to a specific location, he would always choose a route that included as many motorways and main roads as possible, with as few turns as could be achieved. Conversely, I would favour a more interesting route with more bends and scenery. The reason why is that we are different. My dad drives an SUV and hates backroads in case he gets stuck behind a tractor or on roads that are super narrow. He values the reliability of the route over any other metric. I, on the other hand, like to drive. I like to explore the narrow and see outside of the norm. The joy of driving overrides my need for reliability. I just build in buffer time. We both get to the same destination; we may just have taken different routes.

Now, if Matt were going to the same place, he would take a different route again. As an electric car driver, he must ensure he can charge up anywhere on route.

So, three people arrive at the same place, but all three get there differently based on their individual needs. Forcing all three of us to go one route will work well for one of us. One of us would be ambivalent and the other perturbed. But we would all get there (unless Matt ran out of juice!). This is why we have maps – so that we can choose our route – and hopefully, you can now see the analogy.

A sales process will suit some, if not many, but others would be less than impressed. This is why we must shift from the restrictive mindset of a sales process to that of a selling map. We need to allow the buyer to navigate their own path and adapt, rather than the other way around.

This is a no-Sherpa zone

I have a confession. I hate the word 'Sherpa'. This has nothing to do with real Sherpas who help people get to their destination, and I understand, given the gallant role a Sherpa plays, it's easy to parallel what we do in work. It's just been overcooked as a term.

Now, while that is a personal thing, there is something more serious in it. The traditional belief is that sellers act as guides. They assist buyers throughout the selling process to help them navigate their purchase. At each stage of the selling journey, the seller offers support to the buyer. However, the truth is that most sellers are not primarily focused on guiding the buyer; rather, they aim to influence, persuade, and cajole the buyer to take the next step.

But what if that's not really what is going on? What if the buyers are going solo on you? Recent research from firms such as Gartner, Sirius Decisions, IDC, and Salesforce indicates that the buyer is doing just that – completing most of the selling process without you. The actual percentage of the selling process that the buyer participates in can vary depending on several factors, including the complexity of the product or service being sold, the buyer's level of familiarity with the offering, and the buyer's specific purchasing process.

However, today's buyers have greater access to information and resources than ever before, enabling them to carry out extensive research and make informed decisions. It is estimated that buyers typically complete an impressive 80–90% of the sales process independently before engaging with a seller. And AI is making this even higher. According to Forbes, this is up from 57% since 2013 (Forbes, 2014).

This massive change in buyer behaviour is why the concept of a revenue team is so important, and why the Infinite way of thinking is essential for success when we think beyond the single transaction or the simple role of closing.

It should go without saying that if the buyer has changed, the seller's role has to change too. Buyers now have the ability to gather information online, read product reviews, compare prices, and seek recommendations from peers or industry experts. They often enter the sales process already knowledgeable about their pain points, available solutions, and the competitive landscape. This shift in buyer behaviour has led to a higher level of self-education and empowerment, and the moving away from the old selling methodologies that focus on evidencing pain or promoting solutions.

As a result, when buyers *do* engage with sellers, they often have specific questions, seek validation of their findings, or require assistance with more complex aspects of the decision-making process. And sellers must adapt their approach to align with the buyer's journey and provide value beyond the information already accessible to the buyer. We need to provide a map and let the buyer navigate their own journey. We need to provide signposts, rest stops and, if necessary, diversions, but we need to accept that we are no longer in full control and be okay with this.

Yes, I can hear some of you saying we must regain control, or that giving control is the worst thing we can do, but I respectfully disagree. That thinking comes from old thinking and their respecting habits, which is based upon short-term, finite thinking. The evidence from leading research organizations worldwide indicates that buyers prefer a largely seller-free engagement, and those who can provide it will be the most successful. As I have said before, what got us here will not get us there.

It is crucial, therefore, for sellers to recognize and respect the buyer's level of engagement in the selling process. We should aim to be consultative, offering expertise, insights, and personalized solutions that go beyond what the buyer has already discovered independently. We must be prepared to engage with buyers at various stages of their journey, from the initial research phase to the final decision-making stage, and not be limited merely by a two-dimensional, linear process. We can no longer force buyers through our sausage machine of a selling process.

By understanding the buyer's perspective and adapting our selling approach accordingly, we can effectively build trust, add value, and guide the buyer towards making an informed purchase decision. This leads to collaboration and partnership with the buyer rather than simply delivering a pitch. It means we are not just there for a single transaction but for the whole journey. But of course, we need first to understand who our buyer is so that we can ensure that they have the right information available to them when they need it. We need to know our buyers' personas.

Who are you?

As I explained at the beginning of this chapter, different people have varying preferences, which drive diverse behaviours. My dad, Matt, and I all drive, but we each take a different route to reach the same destination, and it's foolish to think otherwise. This is why understanding each persona is so important.

While not new, the concept of personas (or ICPs – Ideal Customer Profiles – if you are in marketing) is still not as widespread as it should be. I am constantly surprised how many organizations have not spent the time developing personas; especially given the impact they can have. So, forgive me if you already know this, but as Matt always says to me, 'Never assume'. Here is some background on personas.

A customer persona, also known as a buyer persona or ICP, is a fictional representation of our ideal buyer, based on research and data about real buyers. We can use this tool to understand target buyers' characteristics, needs, goals, and behaviours. By creating buyer personas, we can better tailor our strategies, messaging, and offerings to engage and connect with our target audience effectively.

Buyer personas typically include a combination of demographic information, psychographic attributes, and relevant details that provide a holistic understanding of the target buyer. Here are some key components commonly included in a buyer persona.

- **Demographic information:** This includes factors such as age, gender, location, education level, occupation, income, and family status. These details help to paint a picture of our buyer's background and basic characteristics. It is worth noting that this can create challenges as well as benefits. With the rightful change in thinking about things like gender, age, etc., we cannot simply pigeonhole people. It can give us clues, but we must be mindful of older thinking that no longer serves us well.
- **Goals and objectives:** Understanding our buyer's goals and objectives is obviously a no-brainer. We can do this by identifying what our buyer is trying to achieve personally and professionally. For example, a buyer persona for a B2B sales process may include cost reduction, productivity improvement, or revenue growth goals.
- **Pain points and challenges:** Now, while I discussed that us trying to expose pain is older thinking, and our buyer probably already knows them, it doesn't mean we should ignore it. Quite the opposite. We need to understand their pains, and buyer

personas should outline the specific pain points, challenges, and obstacles the target buyers typically face. This includes their frustrations, problems, and unmet needs that your product or service can address.

- **Buying behaviour:** This aspect covers how our buyer persona makes purchasing decisions. It can include their preferred channels for research and information gathering, their buying criteria, the influencers or decision-makers involved in the process, and the typical timeline for purchasing.

- **Preferences and motivations:** A good buyer persona will delve into their preferences, motivations, and values. This may include their preferred communication style, content formats, and the factors influencing their decision-making process. Understanding what drives and motivates buyers can help to tailor messaging and offerings to resonate with their needs.

- **Influences and sources of information:** Our buyer personas should also outline the sources of information and influences that impact the decision-making process. This may include online research, referrals from peers (more important than ever before) or industry experts, recommendations from trusted sources, or content consumption habits.

Simple, right? Well, no; actually, it's hard work.

Which probably explains why most organizations don't do it. Creating an accurate and detailed buyer persona requires research and data collection from various sources, including surveys, interviews, market research, and data analytics. And it never stops, as it is important to continually refine and update buyer personas based on evolving insights and market trends. Things change quickly! But it is worth the effort, as using Buyer personas in Sales and Marketing can have a measurable impact on effectiveness in several ways. Let's take a brief look at how it can help.

- **Improved targeting and segmentation:** Buyer personas allow for more precise targeting and segmentation of our marketing efforts. By understanding the specific characteristics and needs of different segments, we can, as I have mentioned before, tailor their messaging, content, and campaigns to resonate with each segment. This leads to more relevant and personalized communication, increasing engagement and conversion rates. When we say the right thing to the right person, at the right time, the engagement is multiplied.

- **Enhanced content creation:** Buyer personas provide valuable insights into target buyers' preferences, motivations, and pain points. This information can guide content creation, enabling us to develop content that speaks directly to the needs and interests of their audience. Tailored content is more likely to attract and engage potential buyers, driving them further along the buyer's journey.

- **Improved lead generation and conversion:** Buyer personas help identify the most effective channels, messages, and strategies to generate leads. By aligning lead generation efforts with the preferences and behaviours of our target buyers, we can optimize lead generation campaigns, increase lead quality, and improve conversion rates. This results in a more efficient use of resources and a higher return on investment.

- **Improved product development:** Buyer personas provide insights into buyer needs and expectations, which can inform product development and innovation. By understanding the target audience, we can develop products or services that address specific pain points and deliver unique value, thus increasing the chances of product success and adoption.

- **Enhanced buyer experience:** And here is the biggest benefit, in my opinion: buyer personas enable us to provide a more personalized and buyer-centric experience throughout the buyer's journey. By understanding buyer goals, pain points, and preferences, organizations can tailor interactions, recommendations, and solutions to meet individual buyer needs regardless of their route, improving satisfaction, loyalty, and the likelihood of repeat business. Now that's infinite!

Have I convinced you yet? I hope so.

When we build our personas, we can start building the map for them. We can understand which route they might take and ensure that all relevant information they need to make a decision is available to them when needed.

All in all, defining and understanding personas, and developing the map, really helps to ensure we reduce the friction in the process.

Fuel or friction: Why deals can stall

I am sure we all understand the importance of reducing friction. Whether it is in the context of making a decision or in the context of physics, reducing friction is largely accepted as a good thing. The interesting thing, though, is that it is often overlooked.

When we face a problem, we often forget that removing friction is more important than adding more power. I can testify to this in trying to open my Victorian sash windows. Too often, I am focused on banging them and swearing at them to move, rather than making a simple adjustment to make them straight to reduce friction. And this is the same in selling. We tend to add to a deal in the hope it will get things moving, rather than seeing what we can take away to make it easier. Let's bring this to life with a bit of theory.

The concept of fuel versus friction relates to the interaction between energy supply and energy loss in various systems. Let's break down each component.

- **Fuel:** Fuel refers to a substance that is consumed to produce energy. In the context of energy systems, fuel typically refers to substances like gasoline, diesel, coal, etc. These fuels are converted into usable energy through processes such as combustion (mostly my temper), chemical reactions, etc.

- **Friction:** Friction represents the resistance encountered when two objects come into contact and move relative to each other. It is a force that opposes the motion of an object, resulting in energy loss in the form of heat and sound (in my case, swearing at the windows!).

In essence, the concept of fuel versus friction revolves around understanding the balance between energy supply and energy loss in a system, and finding ways to optimize efficiency by minimizing frictional losses.

But what about in the context of human behaviour? Here, the concept of fuel versus friction can be applied metaphorically to describe the interplay between motivation (fuel) and obstacles or resistance (friction) that individuals encounter in achieving their goals or desired outcomes. This can be applied to both buyers and sellers in our case, so keep the following in mind.

- **Fuel (motivation):** In this context, fuel represents the internal or external factors that drive and energize human behaviour. It includes various motivational factors such as personal goals, aspirations, desires, values, rewards, or incentives. Fuel can also be derived from external sources such as encouragement from others, recognition, or the anticipation of positive outcomes.
- **Friction (obstacles/resistance):** Friction, in this metaphorical sense, refers to the obstacles, challenges, or resistance that individuals encounter along their path towards their goals. Friction can take various forms, such as psychological barriers (e.g., self-doubt, fear, procrastination) or external constraints (e.g., limited resources, time constraints). It can even be a simple as peer pressure.

The interplay between fuel and friction in human behaviour can significantly impact the likelihood of goal attainment or desired outcomes. When fuel is high and friction is low, individuals tend to be more motivated, focused, and persistent in pursuing goals. They can overcome obstacles more effectively and maintain a higher level of commitment.

Conversely, high friction can act as a deterrent or barrier, reducing motivation and making it harder to achieve desired outcomes. High friction can lead to frustration, demotivation, and even abandonment of goals. Overcoming friction often requires problem-solving, resilience, adaptability, and navigating through challenges effectively.

Table 2   High fuel, low friction

High fuel	👍	👍👍
Low fuel	👎	👍
	High friction	Low friction

As you can see from Table 2, our ideal place is where fuel is high and friction is low. Knowing where we, our deal, and our buyer is on this grid is essential; it should guide us to what we can do to move the deal, as the reason any deal gets stuck is that the balance of fuel versus friction is not right.

As I alluded to at the beginning of this section, the danger is that, in selling, we only seem to have one answer to the problem: add more fuel. I am sure you have been there if you have been in selling long enough, where our manager sees a stuck deal in our pipeline and immediately goes to the place of 'What can we *do* to move the deal?' Does the buyer need a call? Can we give them more information? Can we get a meeting? That might be the right approach, but I have never heard a seller or leader ask what we can take away or how we can reduce friction. It's such a simple paradigm shift in thinking, but it is so very profound, and in the context of the selling process, or now the selling map, it has to form part of our thinking. If we can reduce the friction for a buyer to get to their destination, rather than trying to push them all the time, our results can be transformational. Would you prefer to get to your destination by climbing a mountain or sliding down it?

So, next time a deal is stuck, take a few minutes out to create a little fuel versus friction grid. Work out where the deal is, then adjust towards a place of high fuel and low friction. If you have low fuel and high friction, first move to make changes to encourage low friction, then move to add the fuel.

Table 3   Low fuel, high friction

High fuel	👍	👍👍
Low fuel	👎 ⇨	👍 ⬆
	High friction	Low friction

Like most things we are suggesting in this book, it is not going to be easy as it's going to take bravery to take a different path, but the path less travelled is often lined with jewels, and one thing is for certain, no one ever complains when we remove the friction from them. Here are some practical ways you can look to reduce friction.

- Ensure your value propositions clearly outline the value to that specific buyer/persona.
- Make it easy to contact you for more information.
- Allow your information to be found easily on your website and not hidden behind a complicated structure or paywall.
- If you collect lead information through a form before giving information, only take the minimum necessary information.
- Make buying easy by having clear templates or defining the next steps.

- Pre-empt objections and send the answers to the buyer in advance.

While this list provides a start, there are many other options that could help to reduce friction, and I would strongly suggest taking some time out to focus on this topic and get a list of 10 to 15 options you or your team could use. Some you can implement across all buyers, and some you may want to hold back to use when needed (e.g., objections, as you may raise objections they didn't even have!). You should also notice that I did not include the price here. It's another common mistake we make that as soon as the buyer stalls, we consider if it is the price. It might be, that's for sure; but it should be way down your list of options as it is more likely to be another source of friction.

I was once told a story about a sofa manufacturer who specialized in custom sofas for millennials. They built an amazing website where the buyer could customize their sofa, and they had fantastic studio-style showrooms to allow them to experience the styles. As you can imagine, they were not cheap.

There was an incredible buzz when they launched, and the website and showrooms were full of buyers, but very few people were buying. Curious (and somewhat panicked), the company went about discovering why. Their first thoughts were about price: 'It's too expensive for their target.' Then they thought it might be the experience or there were not enough options to choose from. As this was all conjecture, they did something unusual in most businesses – they actually asked the buyer!! What they found out floored them. It had nothing to do with price, experience, or options. It came down to one single fact: the buyers didn't know what to do with their old sofa! They didn't know how to dispose of what they currently had, and it was stopping them buying.

The manufacturer quickly realized that given they had a delivery van and a delivery team at the buyer's house already, it would be easy to offer a disposal service. On top of that, they could donate old sofas to a charity to help the less fortunate. The result: an explosion of sales with zero cost. Imagine if they dropped their prices and started to discount heavily, or spent a fortune on a new buyer experience.

Take the time to question how you can reduce the buyer's friction. Why not be radical and ask the buyer themselves? I know; crazy, right? That's madness.

The shortest route is not always the best

I am a big fan of revenue velocity metrics. These are the metrics we use to measure our selling motion, and what we encourage other organizations to use to gauge their success. We will dive into these more in Chapter 15, but for now just think of them as leading metrics, or levers, that we can pull to impact selling.

One of the metrics, and one I know is very popular, is time to close. It's the measure of how long it takes for a deal to go all the way from initial contact to close. Now, it's imperfect in many ways, and I will explain that in a later chapter, but what I want to deal with here is the pressure we get to shorten the cycle.

From a pure math perspective, this is absolutely correct. Shortening a sales cycle is desirable, and it means, in theory, you can complete more sales in a period. In theory. The problem, though, is that while shortening the journey is efficient, it is often not effective. In addition, shortening a sales cycle is something we want as sellers but is rarely what the buyer wants.

If we look into the differences between efficiency and effectiveness, we can see that efficiency refers to the ability to accomplish a task or achieve a goal with the least number of wasted resources, such as time, effort, or money. It involves optimizing processes, streamlining workflows, and maximizing output while minimizing input. In the context of work, efficiency focuses on doing things quickly and with minimal waste, often emphasizing productivity and time management.

An *efficient* seller prioritizes completing tasks swiftly and effectively, aiming to achieve specific objectives within tight deadlines.

It has no time or space for the other side of the coin – you know, the buyer!

Effectiveness, on the other hand, emphasizes achieving the desired outcome or result. It involves the ability to produce the intended or expected effects or consequences. Effectiveness looks beyond efficiency and focuses on the quality and impact of actions rather than solely on speed or resource optimization. In our work, effectiveness involves choosing the most appropriate actions, strategies, or approaches to achieve desired outcomes or goals, even if they require more time, effort, or resources. By definition, this *has* to include our lovely buyers. An effective seller considers the big picture, weighs different options, and seeks optimal results rather than merely focusing on efficiency.

Like everything, it's important to note that efficiency and effectiveness are not mutually exclusive, and the optimal balance between the two depends on the specific context and goals at hand. We absolutely need to focus on time to close as a leading indicator, and it's a great place to focus our attention and, where relevant, our coaching, but it needs to be done in balance. Any selling methodology or process that is rigid, that doesn't allow for flexibility or where a company is absolutely focused on a reduction in a metric for the sake of the metric, is not right.

Over the years, I have seen many organizations get a new initiative and double down on sales metrics, constantly pushing for sellers to attain a number without fully understanding that if we take the time to really understand our buyer's challenges and goals, and have real connections with them and are genuinely interested in them rather than just the sale, it absolutely changes the paradigm. Not only does it reduce the friction in the immediate sale, but it also oils the gears for future sales.

And this is why I advocate building 'selling maps', not building 'selling processes'. Processes lock people in and are focused on efficiency. Maps are built with the buyer in mind and are flexible enough to ensure everyone can reach their end goal (even if that goal is with a competitor or doesn't result in a sale at all).

Let's look at how we can build one and connect it to how we work.

Building your map

Let me start with a warning. In writing this section, I realize just how tough it is to explain this process, which is probably the book's most rewritten part. Let's hope I've got this right; if it's not simple, I've failed.

I have used a generic sales process and fictional personas, but please remember that you must adapt this to your process and buyers. Remember, what we are trying to do here is create a place where different personas can travel to the same destination (the sale), but the route can be different for everyone.

Let's do this.

Step 1: Look at your current selling process

Despite my views on selling processes, having one is better than not having one, and they do serve a purpose as it's not the steps that are a problem; it's the order. The rigidity says a buyer has to go through certain gateways to get to the next step. It reminds me of unlocking the next level in a game that has access to certain assets (e.g., a demo or pricing), which only comes after the buyer has jumped through certain hoops.

In this example, I will take a very simple seven-step sales process that is super generic so we can build it out together. Remember, though, to use yours; although, if you haven't got one, this one is a great place to start.

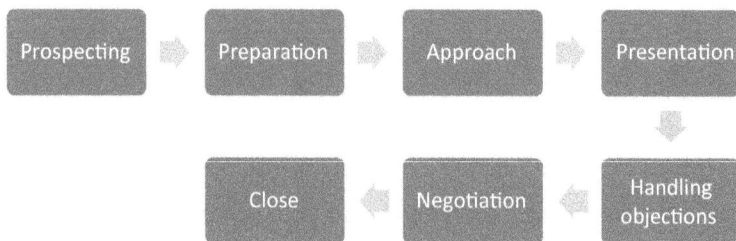

Step 2: Define the activities associated with each stage

Here, we are looking to consider what sales activities are generally associated in each stage. For example, when would you normally do a demo, or give pricing or share the execution plan? So, in our case, this might look like the following (remember to adjust this to your business):

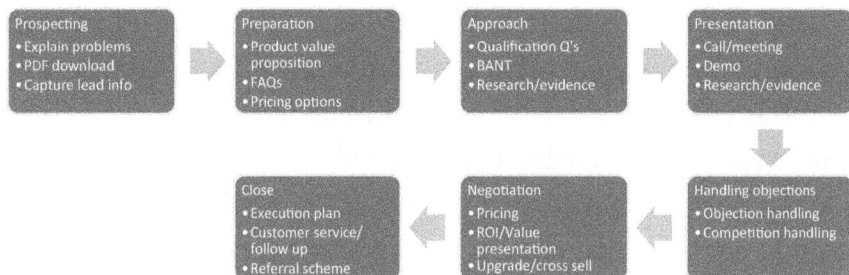

Now, hopefully, you can immediately see the issue. A finance buyer is going to (and this is a stereotype) want to go straight to pricing or the ROI, a technical buyer to a demo, and operations to the execution plan. The problem is that our process doesn't allow for this. You must tick the boxes before we can carry on. Now, I do understand why this might be seen as useful, and there are often some good reasons behind this. Here's two examples.

- You don't want to give out a demo or attend a meeting without first qualifying that the buyer is interested or has the money. No one has time for that.
- You don't want to give out precious information until you have a commitment. Who knows who is asking?

All very valid and absolutely correct. But this approach is very seller-focused and, in a digital world, now largely irrelevant, and this is why. The approach is very binary and doesn't consider the data we should already have on the buyer. It comes from a time when we didn't have data on what the prospect has been doing before asking you. Remember, up to 85% of the sales process above has already been done by the buyer before engaging you. The fact that you, as the seller, are unaware of it, is not the buyer's problem. Forcing the buyer back to a previous stage will frustrate them, and they will start looking for other companies with less friction. Remember, removing friction is more effective than adding fuel.

Let me give you an example from a very recent experience. I was looking to buy software to help us create digital media. I had been looking at five companies, doing my research, and whittling it down to two. This was based on the materials I could find online, and I never spoke to a seller. For the last two, I wanted the pricing to compare the two side by side, as they were essentially the same service.

For company 1, they sent the pricing immediately. For company 2, however, they said that, as they had not yet had a call with us, they couldn't send the pricing until the demo was done. They didn't know that I had watched all the video content on their site and understood the product better than the seller, so I was not going to 'waste' 60 minutes of my time on a demo that I didn't need. Despite my sharing this, the seller absolutely refused to send me pricing. He was sticking to his process and playbook.

Guess what? I bought it from company 1. I still have no idea if it was cheaper, but I do know that I didn't want to buy from any company where they put a process before service – that will never end well.

Step 3: Add points to each activity

In a traditional selling process, we normally assign each stage with a percentage to signify how close the opportunity is to close. In some cases, this is taken further, and that percentage is then used to create a revenue forecast, as you can multiply the order value by the stage percentage.

While this can be a reasonable indicator, it has a problem. The logic is that the further up the sales process the buyer is, the more likely or committed they are to buy. This was probably true before self-service, and buyers ignored our processes and did what they wanted! How dare they!

If you take my example, I was looking for pricing; and in our selling process, pricing is given in the negotiation stage, which is typically 70 to 85% complete in most cases. In their eyes, I was pretty committed. However, I was not at all committed. I was comparing, contrasting, and gathering data, so not at all behaving as the seller planned. It was just a first step.

What we need is a way to measure commitment. The way we can do this is by assigning points to each activity. Points can be weighted, so a demo is worth more points than, say, a download, but I actually prefer to keep them the same. One point for each activity. So, in our example:

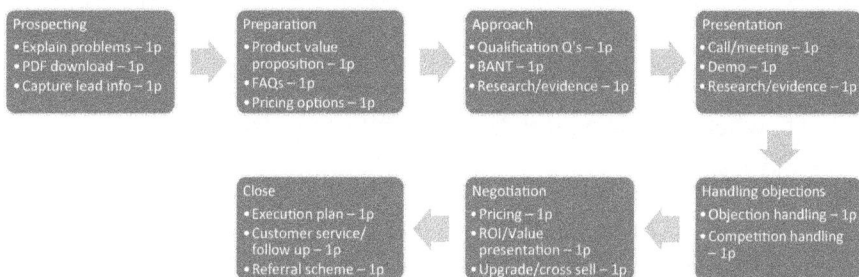

Now this is the foundation for the map. Once we have this, we can create a different view.

Step 4: Build the map

Building the map is a pretty simple task but it allows us to gain some great insights. It will show us:

- how different personas buy;
- which parts of our process are working and which parts are not;
- which activities are worth double downing on, and which could even be dropped; and

- how much of our process is guided by us (sales-guided), and how much is guided by the buyer (buyer-guided).

Not a bad set of insights for a simple tool. As they say, simple doesn't need to mean simplistic. Building it is really as simple as creating a grid. On the x-axis should be the sales stages, just like Table 4.

Table 4   Sales stages

Prospecting	Preparation	Approach	Presentation	Handing objections	Negotiation	Close

Now, for the fun bit: defining the stops and creating routes! To do this, we take the activities we defined for each step and map them out according to their stage and where they might fall, creating a very simple grid of the activities by stage. So, in our example, it would look Table 5, where we have up to three activities by stage.

Table 5   Activities by stage

Prospecting	Preparation	Approach	Presentation	Handing objections	Negotiation	Close
Visit website	FAQs	Incentives to buy	Display evidence	Meeting	Final pricing	Execution plan
PDF download	Value proposition		Meeting	PDF comparison	Payment options	Referral scheme
Intro call	Pricing		Demo	Virtual call	Additional value	

It's important to consider what activities you are providing to your buyers as part of the buying process, as there will be many more than presented here for your business, and three is not a magic number. Equally, just like in 'Approach', it's completely fine to have just one activity in a stage. What's important is that we map them all out so that they are visible in one place.

From here, we can then look to categorize our activities into sales guided (SG) and buyer guided (BG), and add points to each of the activities. Remember, you can add more than one point per activity, although I recommend one each to start with – see Table 6.

Table 6   Buyer-guided and sales-guided activities

	Prospecting	Preparation	Approach	Presentation	Handing objections	Negotiation	Close
BG	Visit website (1)	FAQs (1)	Incentives to buy (1)	Display evidence (1)	PDF comparison (1)	Additional value (1)	Execution plan (1)
	PDF download (1)	Value proposition (1)		Demo (1)		Payment options (1)	Referral scheme (1)
SG	Intro call (1)	Pricing (1)		Meeting (1)	Virtual call (1)	Final pricing (1)	Close (1)
					Meeting (1)		

This part can take time, but it is well worth it as you will also get many valuable insights in fully mapping it out. For example, we normally find that the further towards the close we get, the more focused we are on becoming sales guided. This is what we would expect if we were in the previous paradigm. In modern selling, however, with the buyer wanting to spend as little time with the seller as possible, having lots of sales-guided activities is simply adding fuel rather than removing friction.

This map should help us to think about how the buyers want to buy, more than how we want to sell, and to help us think about what we could deliver as buyer guided rather than sales guided. But it also tells us other things, and this is where the real power of this model is. It shows us the routes different buyers may take and reveals why a sales process is no longer a good reference point for commitment.

For this discussion's sake, we will have two fictitious buyers: Jane and Jack. Jane is an IT director and is a 'technical buyer'. She is focused on how things work and how they will integrate with her current platforms. Jack is the financial controller and is an 'economic buyer'. Jack, like every good finance person, focuses on the price and ROI.

Let's look at Jane's behaviour in the first instance. Her first step is to get the PDF from the website, then look at the FAQs, and then she wants to get a demo before looking at the evidence. Then there is the pricing, and then, if relevant, the closing. If we map this journey out, it looks like Table 7.

Table 7   Jane's sales behaviour

	Prospecting	Preparation	Approach	Presentation	Handing objections	Negotiation	Close
BG	Visit website (1)	FAQs (1)	Incentives to buy (1)	Display evidence (1)	PDF comparison (1)	Additional value (1)	Execution plan (1)
	PDF download (1)	Proposition (1)		Demo (1)		Payment options (1)	Referral scheme (1)
SG	Intro call (1)	Pricing (1)		Meeting (1)	Virtual call (1)	Final pricing (1)	Close (1)
					Meeting (1)		

Note which activities Jane has missed out on, but also notice that she has predominately opted for buyer-guided activities. It is only at the end of the process that she engages with a seller. What a modern buyer she is! If we add up all her numbers, she gets a score of 6.

But what about our friend Jack? His journey is different. He starts, like Jane, with the PDF, but his journey is very different afterwards. This can be seen in Table 8.

Table 8   Jack's sales behaviour

	Prospecting	Preparation	Approach	Presentation	Handling objections	Negotiation	Close
BG	Visit website (1)	FAQs (1)	Incentives to buy (1)	Display evidence (1)	PDF comparison (1)	Additional value (1)	Execution plan (1)
	PDF download (1)	Value proposition (1)		Demo (1)		options (1)	Referral scheme (1)
SG	Intro call (1)	Pricing (1)		Meeting (1)	Virtual call (1)	Final pricing (1)	Close (1)
					Meeting (1)		

Quite different! Again, notice not only what is missing in his journey but also that Jack only required going into three areas, two of which were sales-guided and, in the end, he didn't buy. Did you also note that pricing is sales-guided? Jack has been happy to be buyer-guided for all the steps before, but now he is waiting for a sales-guided conversation, which could be frustrating for him as he cannot move on to his next step until the seller has stepped in. And no doubt the seller wants to validate Jack is a buyer first, so will likely drag Jack back into an earlier qualification step before giving the pricing.

Nine times out of ten, Jack will have discounted you as a seller and moved to another supplier, and that's exactly what he *has* done. Sounds harsh, but that is the reality. Where this may have been acceptable in the past, modern buyers don't have that patience and are looking for those companies that make it easy for them.

Hopefully, you can see how mapping out the journeys should help us to understand what we can do to remove the friction.

But there is more. If we took Jack as the example again, if we were using traditional sales stages to gauge commitment or even forecast value, we would say that Jack is highly likely to buy as he is at the end of the sales process because he is asking for pricing. If we considered the negotiation in the traditional sense, this could be up to 80%. I call BS!

Jack's interest draws him to Stage 6, but that doesn't mean he is that committed; it's just that his activities (his buying preferences) have led him to what we consider to be a place of high commitment. Look again at Jack's points. He scored only 3. Surely, a better measure of commitment is not where the activity is in the process but rather how many activities they partake in.

But be careful! You can find that each persona might have a different buying map, and for that persona a score of 3 is fine, but another (say operations) may need 6. Commitment looks different by persona, which should be no surprise. This is where the traditional model breaks down, as it simply doesn't show commitment in reality.

Modern sales platforms like SFDC and HubSpot can now measure the activity and assign points to activities that help us to understand the journey. And, as best practice, this is exactly what we should be using to measure the commitment of our buyers: buyer activities, not sales processes.

It can take some time and investment to set up, but once done, you have a true understanding of your buyers' commitment and, thus, forecast accuracy increases, which is the goal for everyone because accurate selling forecasts bring significant benefits in planning, delivery, and execution.

I appreciate that not everyone had the ability or tools to have these sophisticated CRM systems in place, but we can measure this using the points we assigned to each step. By simply adding up the activities you know about against the points, we start to get a score that gives us a clue as to their commitment.

It's simple, but flawed. It's flawed by the fact that doing it manually means you need to understand and know when the buyer is taking action. This is fine if it's mostly sales guided, but what about the buyer-guided activity? You would never know. At this point, it becomes guesswork.

This is why investing in and using the right sales technology is no longer optional. Gone are the days when a CRM was for tracking and admin. Today's systems are there to give you insights that help you know where to focus your energy, to help you establish the maps that help you ensure you are buyer focused, not process focused. It can help you to build systems and automations that don't wait for the buyer to make the next step but feeds it to them based on their persona and buyer profile. There is, unfortunately, no longer a one-size-fits-all, and the companies that understand this and execute on it will always be the most successful.

Building these maps and then looking at how your buyers behave is the absolute key to reducing the friction in the selling motion. As we mentioned earlier, we are so used to adding fuel, we forget to reduce the friction. Too many times have I heard leaders advocate for more qualification or more training on selling behaviours like objection handling and negotiation, all borne from the misguided belief that the buyer is stupid and needs everything explained.

Yet, the opposite is true. Provide the information that the buyer needs, when they need it, and get out of their way. Too many sales are being destroyed because we make it hard for people to buy. I can feel myself going into rant mode again, but I am sure you under-stand my point, so I will not linger further on this. Build maps and learn. In summary, there are four steps to follow to start building your buyer maps:

1) Look at your current selling process.
2) Define the activities associated with each stage.
3) Add points to each activity.
4) Build the map.

Before we close out the chapter, it is worth looking at how this whole process can now be simplified with AI. Let's start with personas. While there is a process, it can sometimes feel like guess work. But AI can now mine data from our CRM interactions, email response patterns, webinar attendance and build personas so nuanced they'd make a behavioural psychologist nod in approval. For instance, machine learning might reveal that procurement managers in mid-sized firms prioritize supplier sustainability after 5pm on Fridays, likely triggered by end-of-week ESG reporting. All of this in a fraction of time.

If we also look at the process of creating sales maps, we can also use AI to transform our maps into living systems, as it can adapt based on the persona based on the following.

1) **Predictive routing:** By analysing closed deals, AI could identify which sequences of activities (e.g., case study $\rightarrow$ pricing discussion $\rightarrow$ compliance doc) work best for specific personas. For 'Technical Terry', sending integration docs before demos might shorten cycles by 19 days.

2) **Friction alerts:** Machine learning could flag stalled deals using subtle cues – a drop in content downloads, delayed email replies, or sudden LinkedIn activity around competitors. It's like having a marketing whispering, 'Terry's gone quiet but just downloaded your ROI calculator – nudge him with a client ROI video.'

3) **Adaptive interventions:** When deals plateau, AI could suggest friction-reducers tailored to personas. For 'Cautious Carla', automate a third-party validation report. For 'Time-Poor Tim', summarize key points in a 90-second video.

The point is to use AI to drive even more personalization and adapt in the moment. While this is all possible now, AI offers the ability to automate it, giving us even more time while delivering personal maps at scale.

Remember, 'A map is only as good as its ability to reroute.' If you visit https://infinite.mentorgroup.co.uk/tools, you can download the Buyer Map Creation, which you can use to turn this theory into practice.

Now, all this being said, there is still room for a touch of magic – something that can help us further understand our buyers to help us provide them with the very best service, while ensuring we are protecting our businesses and revenue: the sales methodology!

Chapter 6

The INFINITE methodology

What is a methodology anyway?

OK, so here we go – the meat and veg of what this book is all about: the INFINITE methodology. This is where we aim to bring together all the ideas we have discussed so far to create a sales approach that is suitable for today and the immediate future.

However, let's get some definitions out of the way. When I started to write this, and people were asking me what I was doing, I would confidently talk about the fact that I was writing a 'selling methodology'. Those in sales nodded and thought it sounded good, but those not close to selling asked me to define what a methodology was. And I struggled.

I struggled because, while I have been working with methodologies for some time, I realized I didn't have a good definition, particularly when I compared it to a qualification methodology like MEDDIC (or its variations). So, here we go, let's attempt to make it clear.

A sales methodology and a qualification methodology are two distinct concepts in the way we look at how we sell. While both are important in driving successful outcomes for us and our buyers, they focus on different aspects of the selling process. Let's break them down.

Selling methodology

A selling methodology is a framework that outlines the overall approach, strategies, and best practices for engaging with prospects, moving them through the selling pipeline, and closing deals. It provides a structure or framework for managing the entire revenue cycle, from marketing, through prospecting, to negotiation and closing.

It aims to provide a systematic approach to selling that maximizes efficiency, improves performance, and enhances the overall buyer experience. It guides the selling teams in executing consistent and effective selling strategies.

Qualification methodology

A qualification methodology, on the other hand, focuses specifically on the process of qualifying leads or opportunities to determine their viability and likelihood of converting into successful sales. It involves evaluating and assessing prospects based on specific criteria to determine if they fit the product or service. A qualification methodology helps sellers to prioritize their efforts and allocate resources effectively. It helps identify the most promising prospects and ensures that the selling team focuses their time and energy on leads with the highest potential for success.

A hybrid approach

Here is the crux. These definitions are overly rigid. They originate from a time when selling was more formulaic, there was less change, and outcomes could be anticipated. Back then, you could follow certain steps and get results: A + B = Sales. Not so today. The nature of buyers has changed, and the way they want to buy has changed. The way we engage has changed. So, we must change too. We must change the way we think about selling entirely, and we need to throw out some of what we know. Remember the horses' backsides from Chapter 3? The same is true for methodologies.

For me, a methodology should be more of an ethos, a framework and a way of thinking. I like the word 'framework', particularly as frameworks can be flexible. So far in this book, I hope you will have seen that I have tried to describe the new ethos of selling – something far removed from the previous thinking; an ethos that doesn't require you to have a set of questions up your sleeve or to try to categorize yourself.

When we recognize the value we bring, we should realize we offer much more than simply being a process jockey. We are sellers. We are professionals. We should be proud!

Now, I fully appreciate that there is safety in a process. The step-by-step guided approach can provide great structure for everyone, from those just starting out to those who are further along in their journey, but it diminishes the power of our own creativity and isn't flexible enough to cope when the buyer deviates from the norm, which they are doing more now than ever as they write their own rules in buying.

Unless we are brave enough to let go of our training wheels and our need for structure and bring back the art and professionalism of selling (and I mean this up and down the revenue chain from marketing to sales success), as soon as the buyer doesn't adhere to the plan, we will not know what to do. This isn't a fast-food restaurant where we want to make the burger the same every time. It's time to grow up.

The one area, however, that does need rigour is qualification. This is something that can be split out. It can be defined, and I cannot stress just how important it is. Qualification is the single greatest thing we can do in selling. It matters. It matters a lot. And this is why I am talking about a hybrid methodology. It's the combination of the two concepts that is vital: a framework of selling, with a systematic approach to qualification. They are symbiotic. And like all symbiotic relationships, there are significant advantages over a single approach.

A question I am sure you have asked as you've read the last few paragraphs, is: Why am I so fixated and adamant that qualification is the greatest thing in selling? Well, I shall explain below.

Why qualification matters more than anything else

Qualification is something I was taught early in my career, but it was often regarded as a secondary issue. If sales training had tiers, it would be a tier 3 topic – something viewed as necessary yet not considered core.

When I was at school, I was taught Latin, but after two years of it, the school said that those who failed Latin would have to learn computer studies. Computer studies were viewed as secondary to Latin and almost a punishment. You can guess what I did.

Qualification is rarely seen as super sexy, but in my opinion, it is *the* most important skill we learn as sellers. It sorts out the wheat from the chaff. It's 'magus' (that's Latin for magic!). But it's only magic when used correctly. Used badly, it's useless at best and dangerous at worst.

So why isn't it taught with the same passion as topics like influence or negotiation, if it holds this much power? To be honest, I'm not sure, as it makes no sense not to, but I have a hypothesis and it relates back to our old friend, pride.

Sales qualification, by definition, is the process of determining whether a potential buyer or lead has the characteristics and requirements that make them a good fit for our product or services. It involves evaluating and assessing the prospects to determine their level of interest and likelihood of making a purchase. It should help our teams identify the prospects that are a good match for our offerings, and enable them to tailor our selling approach accordingly.

So, what's wrong with this? Well, look at the language. It focuses on how we justify a prospect as a good match. It helps us stay engaged and identify areas where we might need to improve. And given our own ego, who doesn't like that? When we are with our managers, we like to show why we spend time with certain buyers. However, this is the wrong lens. When I was taught qualification theory, I was taught one thing that has stuck with me forever: Good sellers qualify in, and the best sellers qualify out.

While most of us are using qualification to justify why something is in our pipeline, the best sellers are throwing opportunities out. This is because they know that time is the one thing they cannot control. They only want to spend time working on deals that are actually going to happen, rather than trying to influence and persuade someone who is either not that interested or will be a bad fit. They appreciate that just because they could influence a sale and bring it in, it doesn't mean they should. I can't tell you how many times I have seen people say 'yes' to a deal that they, as the seller, should have said no to, which has cost the company many more times the sale price in buyer support, and even worse, legal bills.

The responsibility for this lies squarely on the shoulders of the leaders; those creating a culture that a strong pipeline should be full of deals rather than strong deals. These leaders seek ways to make a deal fit and pressure the seller to do more. They are, again, adding fuel rather than looking to remove friction.

Any qualification structure, whether the basics like BANT (Budget, Authority, Need, or Time) or more sophisticated ones like MEDDIC (or its many variants), should be used to clean up a pipeline, not to push things through.

The need to focus on qualifying in is created by a lack of understanding and the mindset, as we discussed in earlier chapters, that the pie is finite, and given that we have spent money on a lead, we need to justify it with action.

Not so! We need to use our qualification skills to ensure that we are only working on the right opportunities for us and our buyers. This takes bravery and confidence to say 'no' – 'no' to our managers and 'no' to our buyers. It takes a special state of mind to tell a buyer you're not a good fit. Is it any wonder we promote mental fitness as one of the pillars of today's selling skills?

And this is why we knew that when we were writing this book, we needed to look at a different approach; an approach that was focused on the buyer and the seller in equal measure.

We didn't want a self-serving methodology that only focuses on our needs, but one that considers the buyer's needs. And that's how the INFINITE methodology was born.

INFINITE: It's all in the name

We originally chose the word 'infinite' when considering this project, as it clearly articulated the flow between the buyer and the seller, the relationship between marketing and sales, and it implied growth. Although we liked it, it posed a challenge in developing a suitable acronym for a methodology; however, it ultimately worked out quite well.

The intention is to give you something you can remember and apply to every opportunity to help you understand if you have a real opportunity or need to move on.

So, in this case, the acronym for INFINITE can be seen as:

I   How do we generate **INTEREST**?
N   How can we best establish the **NEED**?
F   How can we reduce the **FRICTION**?
I   How can we understand the buyer's **INTENT** and they understand ours?
N   How can we help them **NAVIGATE** to discover the best solution for them?
I   How can we **INSPIRE** them to take action and the next step?
T   How can we ensure our **TIMING** is right?
E   How can we help them **EXECUTE** on their chosen step?

Those familiar with other methodologies will notice that some elements are similar – Need and Time, for example. This is because they are important to keep, and there is no point in re-inventing the wheel for the sake of it.

You will also notice that on the face of it, you may think this isn't a qualification methodology but more of an approach. That's true, but is also not.

As we look deeper into each one, I will explain (or try to) how you can use this as a framework for selling and a qualification test for opportunities.

AI's transformative impact on sales qualification and processes

As you would expect, sales qualification is experiencing a revolutionary transformation as AI is reshaping how we identify, prioritize, and engage with prospects. Despite the potential for hyperbole, it is actually delivering measurable results across organizations worldwide, fundamentally changing the efficiency and effectiveness of sales processes.

The rise of predictive lead scoring

As discussed already, traditional lead qualification relies heavily on manual processes and our own judgement, often leading to inconsistent outcomes and missed opportunities. Today's AI-powered systems have transformed this approach through predictive lead scoring, which utilizes machine learning algorithms to identify patterns that indicate potential for conversion.

Rather than assigning static points for basic actions like email opens or website visits, AI can examine behavioural patterns, demographic data, and engagement trends to generate dynamic scores that continuously evolve. Companies implementing these systems report improvement in lead quality, with sales teams experiencing significant time savings as they focus their efforts on genuinely promising prospects.

Advanced systems now integrate multiple data sources – including CRM data, website behaviour, email interactions, and even third-party intent signals – to create comprehensive prospect profiles. This holistic approach enables sales teams to understand not only who their prospects are but also where they stand in their buying journey and which specific pain points may be driving their interest. Consequently, the result is more targeted and relevant outreach that resonates with prospects' actual needs rather than generic sales pitches.

Real-time processing and automated workflows

Perhaps the most significant practical impact of AI in sales qualification is the shift from batch processing to real-time intelligence. Modern AI systems can instantly evaluate new leads as they enter the pipeline, automatically routing high-potential prospects to appropriate sales representatives based on territory, expertise, or availability. AI-powered conversation intelligence is also revolutionizing how we can learn from customer interactions. These systems automatically record, transcribe, and analyse sales calls, providing insights into what messaging resonates with prospects and which objections commonly arise. Sales managers can quickly identify coaching opportunities, while individual representatives receive personalized recommendations for improving their qualification conversations. This creates a continuous learning loop where successful qualification techniques are identified, shared, and refined across the entire sales organization.

All said, AI is making a difference, and I would strongly recommend you take the time to learn how to use this superpower to help you more effectively qualify. Remember to qualify out more than you qualify in.

Now onto the INFINITE methodology.

Chapter 7

I – How do we generate INTEREST?

S ome may argue that the greatest question that has eluded humans is the meaning of life (it's 42 by the way – at least according to *The Hitchhiker's Guide to the Galaxy*), but I think the greatest question of all, is obvious: How do we get someone interested in us? Whether trying to attract a partner, establish yourself among your peers, or looking for buyers, the greatest question is: How can we generate interest?

After all, unless there is interest, there will not be a sale. Simple.

In our context, interest can be defined as the curiosity, attention, or desire of individuals towards ourselves, our company, our product, or our services. While focusing on a product or service in this discussion, remember it doesn't have to be just about the product. Interest can be on ourselves and our company as well.

When the buyer's interest is on us, that is when they are interested in the value you bring and is part of the ancient narrative that people buy from people and from people they like. While true, this is not as important as it used to be, especially as we become increasingly digital. But what can be true is that the buyer has seen you or has been influenced by you, driving the decision to buy. There is trust.

A good example for me from my own life is the influence of podcasts. I listen to a *lot* of them and, if I like a presenter, I will often then look to follow their work and then buy their products. The interest is generated by them, and then to their products.

The same can be said about the company. If you are a fan of the company, you become interested in all they do. We can see this with people who follow brands like Apple, or in sports where a fan will buy *anything* with their team's logo on it.

So, keep that in your mind, and I'll share a tool with you later that incorporates this concept further; but in the meantime, let's focus on interest as it relates to products and services.

Interest, if positive, signifies a positive inclination or engagement towards learning more about the product or service, and an increased willingness to explore its features, benefits, or value proposition, and potentially consider its adoption or purchase. This interest can manifest in various ways, such as actively seeking information about the product or service, asking questions, reading reviews, comparing alternatives, or engaging in discussions with others who have experience with the offering. It represents a genuine attraction or enthusiasm towards the product or service, which may be driven by a variety of factors, including perceived need, personal preferences, recommendations, marketing efforts, or specific features and benefits that align with the individual's goals or aspirations. As I said, without interest, there is no sale.

One of the areas that AI is really, really good at, is matchmaking. Given, essentially, this is what interest is (matching a buyer with a seller), AI can accelerate interest-generation by analysing digital footprints (website visits, content downloads) and behavioural patterns to identify prospects primed for engagement. Machine learning models can even prioritize leads exhibiting 'intent signals' – like repeated pricing-page visits or sudden spikes in whitepaper downloads – freeing sellers to focus on high-potential opportunities.

For instance, AI can flag a manufacturing prospect who's researched sustainability initiatives across five sessions, suggesting they're actively seeking solutions. This replaces manual lead-sifting with precision targeting, akin to swapping a metal detector for a GPS. Cool stuff 'if' used properly.

So, how can we use Interest to move our revenue numbers? Well, there are two ways:

1) We can use this to help us generate interest in the first place. Here, we can develop a map that looks at each buyer persona and understand how they might find out about what we do, and then we can overlay our activities to create a heat map. This heat map can then show us where we might need to do more work and where we are currently strong. What is important here is understanding that interest is not one-dimensional. It is highly unlikely that anyone will buy because of one thing we do. It will come through a combination of factors or actions. For more detail on this, please check out our Interest Velocity Interest tool on our website, which you can find by going to https://infinite.mentorgroup.co.uk/tools.

2) We can use it to gauge how interested a buyer might be. Here, we can map the buyer's actual activity and create a score that shows interest. This, again, can be multi-faceted and will be a combination of activities. These can be the steps in the sales map but can also include engagement with us as sellers. The combination

of activity and buyer's communication will lead us to a metric where we can measure interest. This metric can then be used as a qualifier. The higher the number, the more likely the buyer is to buy. To help you create your interest metric, please see the Infinite Engagement Metric tool on our website, which you can find by going to https://infinite.mentorgroup.co.uk/tools.

In summary, understanding interest will help you to know where to go to generate interest and then how to measure how interested the buyer is. It should be obvious, but you will be surprised just how many organizations either don't have or haven't even thought about an engagement metric, and how many don't understand where or how to generate interest.

Chapter 8

N – How can we best establish the NEED (for the product/next step)?

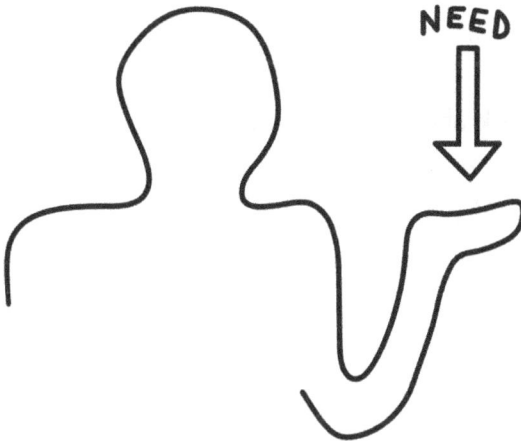

NEED

So, here's one of the oldest and most well-known parts of any sales methodology: understanding the 'need'. It seems so obvious that we need to understand the buyer's need, that it seems almost unnecessary to write anything. I could probably just write 'know the need, and align'. Probably.

However, the truth is that this seemingly obvious element is, in fact, very poorly executed. Most businesses focus on what they need to sell rather than what the buyer requires. They concentrate on how they wish to implement the solution or what they want the product to include, showing very little regard for the buyer.

Before I go further, I want to point out that in some (even many) cases, the buyer does *not* know what they need. When we address a need the buyer isn't even aware of, it leads to tremendous innovation. Apple excel at this – producing products ahead of the market.

Steve Jobs once said, 'Some people say give the customers what they want, but that's not my approach. Our job is to figure out what they're going to want before they do.' But he also said, 'Your customers don't care about you. They don't care about your product or service. They care about themselves, their dreams, their goals. Now, they will care much more if you help them reach their goals, and to do that, you must understand their goals, as well as their needs and deepest desires.'

And this is the balance. We are not going deep enough if we just think about an immediate need. We are not digging below the surface. But below the surface is where the real needs are. Connect to those and magic happens.

When I think about discovering a buyer's need, I try to think of myself as a miner or explorer, searching for clues, digging for treasure, and discovering the real jewels of insight. I have described this many times as the need behind the need. The deeper we go, the stronger the need, and if we can connect to that base need, you will find friction is removed and people will move heaven and earth to meet it, even if that means buying something from you.

As we have discussed in other chapters, AI can transform need analysis by being you miner – mining CRM data, call transcripts, and email threads to detect latent pain points. NLP (Natural Language Processing not the Bandler malarky) could identify recurring themes – e.g., a SaaS client's unspoken anxiety about compliance costs – enabling sellers to address root causes, not surface symptoms.

Predictive analytics take this further, forecasting future challenges buyers might face. Imagine AI alerting you that a retail client's e-commerce traffic will plateau in six months due to seasonal trends – empowering proactive solution-building.

There is a technique I was taught called the 'So what' test. I have also sometimes heard it called the 'Which means' test. Either way, here is a health warning: It is extremely annoying, so be ready and be careful, especially if you are doing this with an actual person. The technique, apart from being annoying, is deceptively simple. You simply think (or ask, if you are brave) of the buyer's need and then ask yourself (or the buyer), 'So what?' or 'Which means… ?' The idea is to get you or the buyer to think what it means if that need is met. It drives the thinking down to the next level. Let me give you two examples: a simple one, and one that's more complex.

Example 1: Buying a sofa

Buyer: 'I need to buy a sofa.'
Us: 'OK, if you get the new sofa, so what?'
Buyer: 'It means that I don't have to look at the dirty old one anymore.'
Us: 'Totally get that! But, so what?'
Buyer: 'When I think about it, it's about how I feel about coming home. I want to feel comfortable and proud of my home.'
Us: 'Yep, I am the same, but again, so what?'
Buyer: 'Ugh! Stop asking me that; it's annoying! Okay, I'll bite. I really want to be proud of my home so I can invite my parents to visit. I want them to be proud of me and the life they helped me create.'
Us: 'Awesome; let's take a look at…'

Yeah, it's a silly example, but we went from knowing they wanted a sofa to understanding why they wanted a sofa. The need to make their parents proud is the real drive and was three layers down in the questioning.

Example 2: Buying a new Business Intelligence (BI) tool

Buyer: 'I am interested in a new BI tool.'
Us: 'OK, great. If you find the right tool, what will it mean to you? What's the "so what?"'

Buyer: 'Oh, that's simple. We will be able to analyse the current production numbers and find out where we could make efficiencies.'

Us: 'Makes sense. I know this sounds like a dumb question, but if you find out where the efficiencies are, so what?'

Buyer: 'If we know where the efficiencies are, we can look to implement a plan to address them and save us money.'

Us: 'Told you it was a stupid question! But indulge me again… If you can save money, so what?'

Buyer: 'Well, that was a truly stupid question! Actually, when I think about it, what it means is that we can improve our cash position, which means we don't have to make anyone redundant despite our downturn in sales recently.'

Us: 'OK, that sounds like a real motivator… Let's take a look.'

Again, a little silly and simplified, but hopefully you can see the point that uncovering need is not about accepting the first need you hear but about digging deeper. You absolutely can do it with the buyer (be mindful of my warning: I suggest practising it on your partner, kids, or pets first so that you can see first-hand how annoying it is if not handled well), but you can also do it with the buyer persona.

While you won't get to the personal needs I highlighted earlier, you will get to the persona and/or company needs. If you then dig for the personal need, you will smash down walls, and their willingness to buy goes through the roof.

'So what?' Two words. Huge power. Huge results.

Want to learn more and put this into practice? Please check out the Needs Discovery tool on our website, which you can find by going to https://infinite.mentorgroup.co.uk/tools.

Chapter 9

F – How can we reduce the FRICTION?

Moving on to F, there was only one choice for where this was going to go. Actually, truth be told, when I first started to develop this methodology, the F was for 'feeling', but as I wrote, I felt that it was both too ethereal (I was starting to knit my own yoghurt again) and not impactful enough.

Don't get me wrong; we know that when we create a feeling, we make a deeper connection, but it was so very close to NEED, it felt like an extension of the same thing and overkill to make a point.

When I was writing about friction and fuel in Chapter 5, it occurred to me that friction is a significantly more important concept for us to consider as part of the methodology. I will not re-write the content on fuel or friction here; you can read that for yourself in Chapter 5, but I will restate the fundamentals.

In any physical movement (and in our case, we are considering the selling motion/journey), you have two choices to get things moving: add more fuel; or remove the friction. In most instances, sellers tend to default to adding more fuel while overlooking the importance of removing the friction.

Adding fuel is easy but consuming and inefficient. Removing friction can be more complicated, but the investment increases efficiency. As an Infinite seller, we are focused on this efficiency. We are focused on looking to remove friction rather than adding more fuel. So, how can we do it?

As I said before, removing friction isn't always as easy as adding more fuel, and in some cases requires great mental fitness as we have to be able let go in places, and where we would normally try to control, we don't. And that's weird.

The art of removing friction starts with identifying where that friction may be, and appreciating that friction for individual personas is different.

A good example of that is meetings. For one persona, attending meetings is vital. They need to look the seller in the eye; they want a discussion. For others, meetings are just two-hour emails and a practical alternative to work.

So, the first step to consider is your process. Look at the buyer journey and map it out just like we did with the maps in Chapter 5. Once we have the steps, look at all the actions required of the buyer and for each persona to establish whether it's friction. We need to see how to reduce or remove it if it's friction. You don't have to remove it completely, but reduction helps. For example, a 30-minute meeting is preferential to a 60-minute meeting.

There is a Friction Identification template on our website, which you can find by going to https://infinite.mentorgroup.co.uk/tools, and it's a great first step to removing friction.

But not all friction is planned. While you can do your best to prep, sometimes friction comes in from a different angle when you are not expecting it. Maybe the buyer leaves the organization during the process, or maybe there is a change in the buyer's finances (real or made up!). Here, we need to sit down and think again about reducing friction, which is why we need to be mindful of it at every step.

We should always ask ourselves how we can reduce the friction for the buyer. What tactics and strategies can we deploy? It should be on our minds as sellers, and a question we should ask our sellers as leaders. It should not just be part of the plan but also part of the response. It is also an excellent criterion for qualification. If we can identify where the friction may lie, we should have confidence that we understand the deal and recognize what is holding it back. Knowing that we can overcome, reduce, or mitigate that friction should instil us with the confidence to pursue the opportunity further.

On the other hand, if the friction is too great, or we can't change it, this could show us that we need to proceed with caution or call it a day and move on. Remember that is *always* an option.

If we don't know or don't have a plan about friction, I would argue we don't know enough, and this should be a yellow or even a red flag. AI can also help you to pinpoint friction points across the buyer journey by analysing historical deal data and real-time interactions. For example, if your prospects consistently stall at contract review stages, AI might flag overly complex legal language as a barrier.

Furthermore, as previously mentioned, AI could predict persona-specific friction: CFOs might prioritize clarity on ROI, while IT directors fear complexity in integration. Customizing communication to these preferences decreases drop-offs.

Now, one final point before we move to the next letter: Removing friction is more important than adding fuel. You should have seen that from earlier. But – and this is a big but – adding fuel and removing friction is when you can go supersonic.

Start with removing friction, for sure. It gives you the best bang for your buck, but once you have removed as much friction as you can, revisit fuel and see what you could add that supercharges the opportunity but doesn't add to the friction. That's how rocket ships are built!

Chapter 10

I – How can we understand the buyer's INTENT and they understand ours?

'Intent' is a word that I have had a fascination with for some time. It's interesting because it is something that really helps us understand another person and/or their behaviour.

It refers to the fundamental purpose or motivation behind their actions, words, or decisions. It involves attempting to comprehend the specific goal or objective a person may have had when engaging in a particular behaviour. Understanding intent can provide us with significant insight into why individuals act in certain ways, aiding us in making sense of their behaviour and predicting their future actions. As you can imagine, this is rather helpful in the selling process.

It's important to note, however, that determining intent is complex, as people's motivations can be influenced by a variety of factors, including their beliefs, emotions, past experiences, and situational context. It can even vary in the moment. As my wife will attest, my intent changes minute by minute, depending on what's happening in that moment (I can be a little impatient sometimes).

While it is not always possible to accurately discern someone's intent with absolute certainty, we can make educated guesses based on available information, observations, and interpersonal communication. In addition, and from the opposite side, intent can also refer to the purpose or objective behind our actions or communication with a potential buyer. It relates to our underlying motivation and the desired outcome they seek to achieve through their sales efforts.

Of course, the intent in selling can vary depending on the situation, who we are, and the organization's goals. Some common intents for us will include the following.

- **Closing a sale:** The seller's primary intent is to persuade the buyer to make a purchase and complete the transaction.
- **Building relationships:** The seller aims to establish trust, rapport, and long-term connections with buyers, recognizing that repeat business and buyer loyalty are crucial for sustained success.
- **Providing value:** The seller's intent is to understand the buyer's needs and offer products or services that genuinely address those needs, focusing on delivering value and solving problems.
- **Creating a positive buyer experience:** The seller's intent is to ensure the buyer has a positive, enjoyable, and seamless buying experience, enhancing buyer satisfaction and potentially generating positive word-of-mouth referrals.
- **Upselling or cross-selling:** The seller aims to increase the buyer's purchase value by suggesting additional products or services that complement or enhance the initial purchase.

It should now be obvious that it is important for the seller to align their intent with that of the buyer, fostering a win–win scenario in which both parties benefit. So, as part of the INFINITE methodology, we need to ensure we are consistently checking in with ourselves to clarify our intent and the intent of the buyer.

Unlike some of the other steps, intent is not something we can assess once for an opportunity and then it's done. As mentioned, we need to check at every step as intent changes. For example, the intent of the buyer to get pricing will be different from the intent of a buyer looking for a demo. And to add more complexity, the intent of one persona for pricing will differ from that of another.

Equally, we need to understand *our* intent for interacting with the buyer at each step, and, again, it should change. But let me give you a clue: If your intent is always to close the deal, you are off track. Yes, that is an admirable goal, but closing a deal is just a by-product of the other intents.

When you add value, demonstrate trust, or build rapport, you are moving closer to that close, which will end up being effortless. This archaic concept (sorry, Mr Baldwin) of 'Always Be Closing' is just not fit for purpose. It's up to us to understand the intents and adapt and match the requirements.

I said earlier it's complex, but with even just a little effort and, most importantly, intentionality, you will be streets ahead of any other seller, as this really gives you an edge. Just thinking about the buyer's intent and your intent, and thinking about what actions or behaviours go along with this is enough to significantly improve your selling performance. It is also incredibly useful for qualification and/or to assess the health of an opportunity. By inspecting any opportunity and seeing how well a seller knows the buyer's intent and their own intent, this will tell you how mature the opportunity is. It can also show you very quickly if you are off track and you and your buyer's intents are off, giving you a chance to course correct or, bravely, qualify out. These are all puzzles that need to be worked out.

As it happens, I'm a big fan of puzzles, but I must tip my hat to AI's ability to decipher buyer intent through sentiment analysis of emails, call tones, and engagement patterns. It's truly impressive. If a prospect's emails shift from enthusiastic to terse, AI can alert sellers to re-engage before disinterest sets in. Conversely, detecting excitement during a demo might indicate readiness to close.

For sellers, AI audits internal intent: Are you pushing for a premature close? Tools like real-time deal scorecards can ensure alignment between buyer readiness and seller objectives.

To help you get an understanding of intents, you will find the Intent Template, which you can use to double down on this skill, on our website at https://infinite.mentorgroup.co.uk/tools.

Chapter 11

N – How can we help them NAVIGATE to discover the best solution for them?

This is going to be shorter than the other explanations for the methodology, as we just spent the entirety of Chapter 5 discussing the need for maps that help us to understand how a buyer navigates through our sales process. And we can use this skill here as part of our methodology as it can be as binary as knowing the persona's likely path or knowing how many points they have racked up to date. The higher the points, the more qualified the opportunity. And if you have read Chapter 6, there is not much more to say. If you haven't read it, stop now and take a look, as it's worth your time.

But worth adding is how we ensure they can navigate to their best solution in the first place. The selling maps discuss how they navigate the process, but it assumes the buyer has already found the basic details of your products and solutions and is on the journey. That's a heck of an assumption.

Now there are two sides to this, as a buyer needs to be both receiving your offering and understanding it. Marketing 101, right!?

It might be 101, but 99% of the companies we work with don't do this. Well, that's not entirely true and a bit harsh; what we see is this:

1) They are focused on one thing but not the other (e.g., really strong value propositions but poor delivery to the buyer).
2) They do it, but for one solution.
3) They do it, but for one persona.

The reality is we need to invest our time in making sure we know how and what we are sending out to a client, and then using some of that old-fashioned marketing theory (not everything is garbage) and making sure our message has as many eyes on it as possible.

Here is where the other elements of INFINITE start to collide, as we start to build a picture and a demand generation strategy (I use this term rather than 'marketing strategy', as this is what marketing is for – generating demand; sometimes we forget that simple fact.), based upon their needs, intents, etc.

As discussed in Chapter 5, it's also worth remembering that AI-powered journey mapping tools can analyse past deals to predict optimal pathways for specific personas. A healthcare buyer might follow a compliance-heavy route, while a startup prefers rapid prototyping. AI can dynamically adjust content recommendations – ROI calculators for CFOs, case studies for end-users – keeping engagement relevant.

The point of navigation is to know where you are going and where the buyer will go. Then, with that knowledge, adjust and adapt.

Check out the Selling Map Creation tool on our website, which you can find by going to https://infinite.mentorgroup.co.uk/tools, as it's incredibly powerful both as an insight generator for demand generation and, when combined with the concept of the point, the core for your understanding of how well qualified an opportunity is and even your forecasted revenue.

Chapter 12

I – How can we INSPIRE them to take action and the next step?

In most books on selling, we talk about getting the buyer to take the next action. We teach buyers that if we can get an agreement on the next step, it will create an agreement for them to take action. This is fine and largely a reasonable approach. But it's missing something.

Often, the next actions are something the buyer is being forced (or cajoled) into. They have to do this step to get the next thing, the thing they probably want. For example, if I want to get pricing, many companies hide their pricing until they can get you on a call or a demo.

Therefore, as a buyer, I am forced to take an action I don't want/need in order to get what I want. Adding fuel.

Equally, in our process-driven approach, we then mark them as more engaged or further qualified as we believe their acceptance of the action is a buying sign. Again, I call BS. Remember, in our earlier example, the buyer only completes the action because they want something else. The alternative approach is to inspire the buyer to take the next step.

It may sound like a platitude or a fluffy term, but let's look at the definition of the word. 'Inspiration' can be defined (and I like this a lot) as a powerful and stimulating force or influence that arouses creative thought, motivation, or action. One definition might be: a spark of ideas. It can also suggest enthusiasm that moves us to pursue our goals and consider new possibilities. Inspiration can lead us past a range of perceived limits through creative and innovative thinking.

By inspiring our buyers into action, we are creating a highly charged, highly positive environment that drives real change and can be a huge competitive differentiator. I can guarantee, unless they are also Infinite sellers, your competition is unlikely to be thinking in terms of inspiration. From our initial prospecting through to customer success (the Infinite Loop), we need to be thinking about how we inspire our buyers to take action.

So, how do we do this? Like most things, first, we need to be aware it's something we need to do, and be intentional with our actions, but there are some practical things too. Here are some strategies to inspire people to take the next action.

- **Understand the target audience:** Yeah, okay, common sense, but sadly not common practice. We need to research and analyse our target audience to gain insights into their preferences, lifestyles, and pain points. With this, we can understand how best to inspire as we connect what we do with what the buyer needs or wants (two very different things).

- **Focus on the benefits:** Again, from Sales 101, we need to ensure we are clear on what our product or solution solves for the buyer, rather than its features. This has been taught for as long as I have been in enablement but is still poorly executed by 90% of sellers.

- **Create an emotional connection:** Matt always says that people buy for just three reasons: to save something, solve something, or increase something. This is sage advice, but underneath all of that is the understanding that there is really only one reason anyone buys anything: to deal with an emotion. Practically speaking, we need to tap into people's emotions by telling compelling stories, using relatable scenarios, or showcasing real-life examples and connecting the product or service to their aspirations, happiness, or well-being, making it more appealing and meaningful.

- **Demonstrate social proof:** Buyers love proof. They love to review reviews and find out how other people have had success (or not). Today, with the huge increase in review sites and the desire to self-serve the sales process, ensuring our buyers can get social proof of our benefits is more important than ever. We should look to incorporate testimonials, reviews, and success stories from satisfied buyers. Positive experiences shared by others can build trust and create a sense of credibility, influencing potential buyers' decisions.

- **Offer personalized experiences:** This is huge and connects with the paradox that buyers, while wanting to self-serve generic data to find a solution, also want a personalized experience. Thankfully, leveraging data and technology to personalize the buying experience, tailor recommendations, and deliver messaging based on individual preferences, previous purchases, or engagement history, is doable.

- **Use persuasive visuals and storytelling:** One of the hardest but most powerful things we can learn to do is tell stories. There are many books on this topic, and we teach this a great deal with our clients, but the ability to tell a story is one of the multipliers that is largely overlooked and sadly underused. We should utilize high-quality visuals, captivating videos, or engaging narratives to create an immersive and memorable experience. Appeal to people's senses and imagination to make the product or service more enticing.

There are other ways (which I will add in the following list for balance), but these all feel a little 'Napoleon Hill' (an American self-help author; he is best known for his 1937 book *Think and Grow Rich*).

- **Provide a sense of exclusivity or scarcity:** Create a perception of exclusivity or limited availability by offering special editions, limited time offers, or access to exclusive benefits. This can create a sense of urgency and drive people to take action. This is fine if it's real, but the flip side is when buyers realize we are creating artificial scarcity; it can backfire, and we lose trust.
- **Offer incentives:** Most people are coin-operated, so providing incentives is a proven method. We can provide incentives such as discounts, freebies, or loyalty rewards to incentivize action. This can enhance the perceived value and motivate people to make a buying decision, but it feels a little cheap. We will be adding steak knives and shouting, 'Wait, there's more...'

Inspiring people to take action goes beyond simply promoting the product or service. It involves understanding and connecting with buyers emotionally, demonstrating value, and effectively addressing their needs and desires.

From a qualification perspective, we should look to be rating our buyers' inspiration. It can be subjective, but a simple 0–10 rating can give us a RAG (red, amber, green) status of how inspired a buyer is and, therefore, what we might be able to do to drive inspiration up.

Can AI help us here? Certainly, AI elevates inspiration from transactional nudges to strategic momentum. Full disclosure: AI wrote that last sentence and even I don't know what it really means, but I left it in to make a point that for AI to help us inspire our buyers, don't leave it to its own devices!

However, in this context, AI can help at this stage of the process by correlating buyer behaviours with historical wins; it suggests tailored success stories – e.g., sharing a sustainability-focused case study with a prospect who's lingered on ESG (Environmental, Social and Governance) pages. Chatbots handle initial FAQs, freeing sellers to add real value. At least that's the premise.

Check out the Inspiration Window tool on our website, which you can find by going to https://infinite.mentorgroup.co.uk/tools.

Chapter 13

T – How can we ensure our TIMING is right?

Time to hit you up with a couple of widely available quotes (I think I have avoided them so far!). Here we go:

'The right thing at the wrong time is still the wrong thing.'

Joshua Harris

'Life is all about timing... the unreachable becomes reachable, the unavailable becomes available, the unattainable... attainable. Have patience. Wait it out. It's all about timing.'

Stacey Charter

Yes, they are 100% cheese, but these quotes emphasize the significance of timing in various aspects of life and how it can impact our experiences, opportunities, and outcomes.

Timing plays a crucial role in selling. In the sales world, recognizing the right moment can make the difference between closing a deal and losing a potential buyer. The significance of timing extends beyond merely reaching out to prospects or presenting a product or service (although there is nothing more wonderful than speaking to a client who is just about to buy something else!). It encompasses the entire Infinite revenue process, from lead generation to negotiation, closing, and renewal.

Let's go through the cycle. First and foremost, timing impacts lead generation and prospecting. Identifying potential buyers at the right time increases the chances of success. For example, reaching out to prospects when they are actively seeking a solution to their problem, or during a period of change in their business, can significantly improve conversion rates. By targeting prospects at the right moment, sales professionals can establish a connection based on relevance and address their needs effectively.

As we move around to the middle of the cycle, timing is just as crucial during the initial offering. Presenting a product or service when the prospect is most receptive and engaged can significantly impact the outcome. We need to recognize the buyer's readiness to listen and ensure we are providing information that aligns with their current concerns or goals. By adjusting the timing of the presentation to match the prospect's mindset, we can increase the likelihood of capturing their interest and attention. Heck, we might even inspire them!

Next up, negotiation. It's essential to strike a balance between being assertive and respectful, and this requires a keen sense of timing. Recognizing when to keep negotiations going, when to walk away, and when to hold firm can significantly impact our negotiation success. The right timing allows us to navigate the negotiation process effectively, ensuring that everyone feels satisfied with the outcome. Remember, think about expanding the pie, not just sharing one. Knowing when to increase the pie is where the magic happens.

And then there is closing. It should be obvious but closing the sale is another critical moment where timing plays a decisive role. Attempting to close too early or late can cause horrible outcomes (I have scars). We should gauge our buyer's readiness to decide and seize the opportunity to inspire them to take the next step. Waiting too long may give the buyer a chance to reconsider or explore other options, while closing too early can create a sense of pressure and push the buyer away. We can maximize our chances of successfully closing the deal by using the right timing.

Finally, timing also affects long-term buyer relationships as we move to the end of the loop and go beyond individual sales transactions. Knowing when and how to follow up with buyers is essential for building trust, maintaining communication, and fostering loyalty. Regular check-ins and appropriate timing of upselling or cross-selling opportunities can help nurture buyer relationships and drive repeat business and renewals.

The importance of timing in selling cannot be overstated. From lead generation to closing deals and fostering long-term relationships, the ability to recognize and take action at the right moment can significantly impact our success.

Those of us who master the art of timing understand our buyers' needs, adjust our approach accordingly, and take the opportune moments to connect, engage, and close deals. Sellers can enhance their effectiveness, build strong buyer relationships, and achieve their sales objectives by considering timing as a strategic element in the selling process.

The reverse action plan is one of the most powerful tools we can use. This tool (you can find it on our website, at https://infinite.mentorgroup. co.uk/tools) enables you to see what actions you want to inspire the buyer to take, and you work backwards from the transaction timing. It encourages you to think about when each action should happen. If you have never tried it, you need to. It's a game-changer!

Remember, as Joshua Harris said, 'The right thing at the wrong time is the wrong thing.'

Chapter 14

E – How can we help them EXECUTE on their chosen step?

Unless you have been asleep reading this far (and who could blame you), you should be clear on my view that we need to remove friction rather than look to add fuel, and this is what we are talking about here in one of the most overlooked areas in selling – the execution.

In our business, we sell revenue transformation, and we are pretty good at it.

It can often be complex, but we know how to inspire our buyers to take the leap to address their revenue transformation challenges; however, it wasn't always that way. We were always pretty good at the whole value equation stuff. Demonstrating what we do has tangible ROI, and every £ spent with us meant £££s in the buyer's pocket. We knew how to evidence it, record it, and use great metrics (more of that in the next chapter) that allowed people to measure it. But despite this, we were often overlooked at the end of the cycle. It turned out that the reason was super simple, just like the simple solution the sofa company discovered in Chapter 5. Well, a simple *reason*, but it certainly was not a simple fix.

We found that the buyers were pleased with the solution and satisfied with us as a credible provider; however, they were unclear about how we would carry out the delivery. Oh sure, we gave a delivery roadmap, examples of enablement sessions, etc., but we did not give the buyer a full view of what would happen next. Our presentations and value propositions were 85% about convincing the buyer that what we were proposing was good, and the other 15% was either commercial or testimony. So, we had to fix that and start to ensure that when a buyer engaged with us, they would know exactly how we would execute this.

I know you are shouting at me now that this makes sense for complex services solutions like revenue enablement, but you sell widgets. Fair shout, you're right. And you are 100% wrong.

Let's go to the other end of the extreme and look at selling shoes over the internet. To be precise, running shoes. As a runner myself, I know this world pretty well and have bought from dozens of different shops, and the ones I return to understand that it's more than just delivery that's important. They understand I want to know what will happen and what happens if what they say will happen does not happen. That's a lot of 'happens'.

Most retail organizations now give you the ability to track a package – that's table stakes – but they leave the experience of understanding the next steps to the courier, and here in the UK, couriers could do better. Why would you delegate that responsibility, which is so critical to the experience, to the people with the lowest ranking customer feedback ratings (they are only outranked by British MPs in low customer satisfaction, but that's another book and story if we ever meet for a beer)?

The message here is that we need to be as mindful and intentional about building out an execution plan as we are about ensuring we demonstrate value. We need to make sure every stakeholder knows what happens when they buy.

Surprises are for birthdays (personally, I would say not even then) and not something enjoyed in selling, particularly after the transaction has happened, and so it is our responsibility to be clear about every next step. And we need to be thorough. This is not just (although largely) about how we may implement or deliver a solution, but it's also clear about the steps needed before that. For example, a contract needs to be signed, data needs to be gathered, meetings need to be had, and time needs to be spent. If you are not clear, the buyer has to guess. And if they have to guess, they make assumptions. And that's not good.

I remember we bought a professional services automation solution (or PSA), and while we knew it would not be easy, the actual investment in time and resources was significantly higher than we thought. This led to the feeling of dissatisfaction during the implementation, at least one resignation, and a desire not to recommend them in the future.

Truth be known, given the scale of what we were doing (ripping out and replacing the admin heart of the business), it was always going to be hard, but it was sold that it would be easier than it was.

If the supplier was honest with the actual effort that was involved, it might have persuaded us to go elsewhere, but probably not as their solution was the right one; however, it would have set expectations that would have reduced the stress and affected our overall happiness with the project, and probably more recommendations and more business.

If you have something complex to convey, strive to simplify it. However, most importantly, remain honest. If you have something simple to deliver, don't assume it's simple to the buyer. Make it clear how you are going to execute, and do it early. It's a huge differentiator.

From a qualification perspective, if you have not explained or do not have an execution plan for what you are selling, you could be subject to a hidden objection that can bite you on the rear (like it did for us). If there is no plan to execute, the buyer is not qualified. Now, equally, if the buyer objects to the execution plan (and this could be for various reasons, including legal, practical, financial, or time), you want to know early to qualify out.

Post-sale, AI can help to ensure seamless execution by automating onboarding workflows and predicting roadblocks. If a client's IT team historically struggles with API integrations (never heard of that before!), AI can pre-emptively schedule training sessions and share troubleshooting guides. Real-time feedback loops then refine future processes.

Creating an execution plan will depend on what you sell, but you will find a few examples on our website, at https://infinite.mentorgroup.co.uk/tools.

Crazy context

'But wait,' I hear you cry, 'aren't a tonne of things missing from your methodology? Where do you talk about value or even who to speak to? You have not even mentioned the economic buyer or champions!'

Yep! Spot on. This might be heretical, but I am going to say it anyway: Those topics are valuable, but in the business of selling, especially after 50 years of it being pushed at us, they are very well understood and are table stakes. These things are the basics. When I started to write this methodology, I deliberately avoided these topics for two reasons:

1) I wanted something that was deeper and spoke to the issues facing selling today, not from the 1970s.
2) For me, these topics are contextual; they differ in importance depending on who you are, what you sell, and how you sell it.

I wrote INFINITE to transcend the concept of complex sales versus transactional sales, which spoke of more than value or solutions selling, and to be something that could challenge any seller.

Of course, ensuring we add value is important, and, of course, making sure we are speaking to the people who hold the budgets is critical, but if you follow the INFINITE steps and ask yourself the questions against each letter and then apply your context, you will cover these anyway.

And a whole lot more.

And that's my point. The structure of INFINITE and the questions and tools are there to help you over the whole loop, the whole cycle. They are there to avoid a soulless process or sausage machines, resulting in poor buyer experiences and, thus, no longevity.

The methodology can and should be applied to every manner of sales and also to the context of partners and channels where appropriate. The context may change, but the core principles work regardless.

I understand we need to scale, but we scale today through technology, which means we can avoid vapid transactional mindsets that don't require us to think but simply follow the battle card (don't get me wrong; apart from the name, which is a throwback for a different era, battle cards can be very useful as prompts). It allows us to respect our buyers enough to have their best interests at heart and ours too, as we work together in partnership.

I also fully understand that embracing the INFINITE methodology and mindset will require a paradigm shift, and that not everyone will agree or be willing to make the necessary changes and sacrifices. That's totally fine – you do what you need to. Haters will hate, and the world will continue to spin.

For those of us who dare, though, there's another level of revenue success, personal satisfaction, and joy that can be found in the noblest of professional selling.

Remember, context is everything. EVERYTHING.

Part 3

Infinite results, endless flow

Chapter 15

Measuring the results

R enowned management consultant Peter Drucker is attributed with the creation of the famous quote, 'What gets measured gets done'. Although the exact wording may vary slightly, the essence of the quote emphasizes the importance of measuring and tracking progress to ensure that tasks and goals are accomplished effectively.

It is a phrase I first encountered while consulting for a large retail organization that had just begun collaborating with an outsourcing partner. This partner was assessed based on their actions and compensated according to those results. We were surrounded by balanced scorecards, KPIs, and metrics. And Peter Drucker was proved right. The elements we measured were not only completed but also improved. In contrast, those elements to which we did not devote as much time did not show the same progress.

A few decades later, I remain incredibly grateful for that experience, and I continue to be a strong advocate of the principle – so much so that it's worth writing a chapter on it. Let's be honest: metrics and results aren't naturally our focus.

Well, that isn't entirely true, of course. We all excel at focusing on 'the number'. Whether that is our target, the company targets, or another lagging indicator, it's what drives most conversations. And so it should. If you do not know where you are, you cannot determine what actions to take to influence it. Furthermore, being 'data-driven' is now a critical aspect of our roles.

What many of us tend to forget is the significance of measuring *leading* indicators instead of concentrating on the *lagging* ones. Leading and lagging indicators are two types of performance metrics that provide different perspectives on our performance and can help us to assess the effectiveness of our strategies and tactics.

Leading indicators

Leading indicators are forward-looking metrics that provide insights into activities or behaviours that are expected to drive future results. They are often considered predictive in nature, as they indicate the likelihood of achieving desired outcomes. Leading indicators typically focus on activities that occur earlier in the sales and marketing process. Examples of leading indicators in our context may include:

- the number of qualified leads generated;
- conversion rates at various stages of the sales funnel;
- website traffic and engagement metrics;
- social media engagement (likes, shares, comments);
- email open and click-through rates; and
- number of product demonstrations or presentations delivered.

By monitoring our leading indicators, we can proactively identify potential issues or areas of improvement, adjust their strategies, and take corrective actions to maximize future performance.

Lagging indicators

Lagging indicators, on the other hand, are retrospective metrics that measure outcomes or results that have already occurred. They are often seen as a reflection of past performance. Lagging indicators are typically focused on the final outcomes of our revenue efforts. Examples of lagging indicators for us may include:

- total revenue realized;
- number of deals closed;

- average deal size;
- customer acquisition cost (CAC);
- return on investment (ROI); and
- customer satisfaction ratings.

Lagging indicators provide a retrospective view of the success or failure of our initiatives. They are useful for assessing overall performance and measuring the impact of strategies and campaigns.

The relationship between leading and lagging indicators is that leading indicators can provide early signals or warnings about potential changes in lagging indicators. By closely monitoring leading indicators and making adjustments based on their performance, organizations can influence and enhance lagging indicators.

When I explain this to most people, I often use a sporting analogy, as it helps bring it to life. The challenge with sporting analogies is that they can be cultural, so I will use one that is acceptable in most parts of the world: soccer.

Our lagging indicators, in this case, are things like the final score (1–0, 0–3, etc.). From this, we know whether we won or lost. We can then review the game and find out what we did right or what we could improve on. This is useful.

But it's only useful for the next game.

Our leading indicators, however, could be something like shots on target or ball possession. This can tell us during the game how we are doing and allows us to think about what we can do to adapt. We can literally change the game outcome mid-way. Matt and many of my colleagues are far more qualified than me to regale you of stories when a change in tactic or player changes the game.

This sounds fantastic, but it necessitates systems and discipline, which is why I am such a fan of revenue management systems like our own (visit www.mentorgroup.com for more info) and the impact they can have on revenue across any organization in any context.

From chaos to calm

As an organization, we have been building and delivering revenue management systems for over a decade and have seen some incredible results for buyers.

A revenue management system is simply a way of bringing structure and order to best-practice, revenue-generating meetings, focusing on creating consistent results, and the results from our customers are simply outstanding when a system is applied.

It brings calm to chaos. It also brings together everything we must do to generate revenue and makes it something we can do without stress.

Observationally, much stress surrounding revenue generation stems from its unpredictability. One of the funniest statistics I have heard came from CSO Insights (CRM, 2016), which compared forecast accuracy to roulette. Your chances of winning at roulette were 47.5%, while your average forecast accuracy was 46.5%. Crazy!

This is often created by the lack of structure of how sellers' managers demand generators and create campaigns, and their managers manage the work. The meetings are often unscheduled, have a different structure each time, and are not data driven.

Add to that the pressures of quarterly results, and what we find is little discipline until the last two weeks of the quarter, and then craziness as people scramble to get to the number.

And, of course, by then, it is too late to really do anything profound, so you get unhealthy behaviours kicking in, like sandbagging (avoiding putting deals in a CRM so they have something in their back pocket), pushing deals, pulling deals and, in the worst cases, downright fabrication.

The better way is to put in something predictable. Something where everyone knows what to do, when to do it, and has accountability from the start. Utopia!

While there are not many unicorns and rainbows in selling, a well-executed revenue management system is pretty close. Let's break down the components of a revenue management system so that we can bring it to life.

Dashboards

You may have guessed by now, but I love my data. I enjoy nothing more than looking over data for trends and insights that can help buyers move the needle. But I am also aware this is an unusual passion for revenue generators. Let's be honest; most people look blankly at spreadsheets and tables and glaze over. And this is where good dashboards can come in. They should, if designed right, provide the viewer with several things, as in the following.

1) **Clarity of what's important:** A good dashboard should only provide you with a summary of important data, like your dashboard in a car. In a modern car, the oil pressure is not important, so the dial no longer appears on most cars. Your speed, however, is important, so it is normally the largest dial in front of you. Dashboards cut out the clutter so that we can focus only on the details.

2) **Consistency:** Data can be tough to interpret, and what one person sees in it differs from another. A good dashboard will ensure that everyone looks at the same data similarly. Sure, they can slice and dice it differently if they want, but the core metrics and data points are consistent across your teams. Everyone is seeing the same measures. There are many cracking cautionary tales of where it goes horribly wrong when teams are using different metrics on the same projects. From bridges that don't line up (feet versus metres), to planes running out of fuel (gallons versus litres), it's a horror show.

3) **Accountability:** Data can be wonderfully transparent, meaning that the data is what it is. There is no denying the numbers or the details. Data can indeed be manipulated, but with the

right checks and balances, and good data discipline, it is what it is. A seller can tell you that they are calling buyers daily, or demand generators can say their campaign is a runaway success, but if the metrics tell you differently, you can hold people to account. Just remember, though, the old saying of 'garbage in, garbage out' is universal, so good data behaviours and adoption are key to success.

I must be careful here as data, while awesome, can be very dangerous. Measure the wrong things and you can be in a very difficult position and make some very bad decisions. The best advice is to work with people that know data. And make this a priority. Why? Simply put, data-driven revenue organizations perform better. Standby for stats:

- **Improved revenue:** According to a study by the Aberdeen Group (Aberdeen Strategy & Research, 2016), companies with strong sales and marketing alignment, driven by data, achieved an average of 20% annual revenue growth, while companies with poor alignment experienced a 4% decline in revenue.
- **Enhanced retention:** A study from the Centre for Mental Health, quoted by Gartner (2024) revealed that companies using advanced analytics for customer experience saw a 5–10% increase in retention rates and a 10–15% increase in revenue.
- **Increased sales productivity:** According to a Harvard Business Review study (Gartner, 2025a), organizations that effectively used data and analytics in their sales process experienced a 5–6% increase in sales productivity.
- **Improved lead conversion rates:** A study by Marketo (Marketo, 2021) showed that companies using data-driven strategies and analytics to segment and target leads achieved a 50% higher conversion rate than those that didn't. Get Data. Use Data. Fly!

Regular meetings with a consistent agenda

Anyone who knows me understands I like structure. I prefer my bag packed in an organized manner, and if something isn't in the diary, it doesn't exist (seriously, I schedule E V E R Y T H I N G). Therefore, it's not surprising that I advocate for having regular meetings with a fixed agenda.

However, thankfully, it's not just me. Research and surveys conducted by giants like Harvard Business Review, Gallup, and McKinsey have underscored the significance of effective meetings and structured communication in achieving positive outcomes related to productivity, decision-making, and employee engagement. What are they, I hear you ask? Let's take a look, and you will see some common themes.

- **Increased productivity:** Regular meetings with a fixed agenda help to structure discussions and keep participants (revenue generators normally have the attention span of goldfish) focused on relevant topics. Having a clear agenda and time allocation for each item makes meetings more efficient, reducing unnecessary tangents or unrelated discussions. This leads to increased productivity as time is utilized effectively. We talk about content, cadence, and compression, as one of the first objections from people is 'Oh no, not more meetings'. Done well, structured meetings *reduce* the time spent due to the focus. No, seriously, they do – I have evidence.
- **Improved communication:** Fixed agenda meetings ensure important information is shared consistently among team members. It provides a platform for everyone to contribute, ask questions, and provide updates on their work. This fosters better communication and ensures that relevant information is disseminated to the appropriate stakeholders.
- **Better decision-making:** When meetings follow a fixed agenda, decision-making becomes more structured and objective. Each

agenda item is discussed thoroughly, allowing for a systematic evaluation of options, weighing pros and cons, and reaching a consensus. This helps avoid impulsive or uninformed decisions that can arise in freeform management.

- **Alignment and clarity:** Scheduled meetings with a fixed agenda enable teams to align their efforts and work towards common goals. The agenda can include items related to overall strategy, priorities, specific accounts, and revenue targets, ensuring everyone is on the same page and working towards shared objectives. This clarity minimizes confusion and promotes a cohesive team environment.
- **Accountability and progress tracking:** A fixed agenda, as mentioned earlier, can include items for reviewing progress, setting targets, and assigning responsibilities. This promotes accountability among team members as they must report on their progress and deliverables. It should, with data, provide us with information early enough that we can actually take action!
- **Lasting behaviour change:** Fixed meetings can also drive lasting behaviour change and the right leading activities between meetings. This is because the agenda drives the outcomes, and if the behaviours are not delivering the required outcomes, the behaviours are often adapted to make sure they do.

Meetings can be weekly, monthly, or quarterly depending on what you want, and there is an entire book to be written on the best practice meetings you can have. The point is to build the meetings, schedule them, and stick to them. It's super simple really, but it can be harder to execute as you herd the cats. Stick with it; the results will follow.

Mentoring

I will cover this topic more in the next chapter, so I will not labour the point too much here, but the other element of any revenue management system is mentoring.

In my world, mentoring refers to a relationship in which an experienced seller or leader provides guidance, support, and advice to a less experienced seller to develop their sales skills, knowledge, and overall effectiveness – hand-holding if you like, but with a bit more purpose.

The mentor (typically) possesses more experience and expertise in either the product/solution or in selling in general. The purpose is to share their knowledge, insights, and best practices to help the mentee enhance their selling abilities, overcome challenges, and accelerate their professional growth.

Sales mentoring can also benefit both the mentor and the mentee. The mentee gains valuable knowledge, skills, and insights from the mentor's experience, enabling them to improve their performance and achieve greater success. Meanwhile, the mentor can share their expertise, contribute to developing emerging selling talent, and potentially gain fresh perspectives and ideas through interactions with the mentee.

Win–win. Actually, win–win–win – if the mentor and mentee win, everyone wins! According to a study by the Sales Management Association, companies that provide effective mentoring can see up to a 16.7% increase in revenue. That's hard to ignore!

Those of you familiar with this topic might be asking why I am talking about mentoring when everyone else talks about coaching. Glad you asked, but check out Chapter 16 for that chestnut! The bottom line here is that a combination of dashboards, meetings, and mentoring is one of the keys we have seen to transforming your revenue, and why Mentor Group have been developing and executing these with extraordinary results.

The 3 Vs

We discussed earlier the benefits of measuring leading over lagging indicators, and now I want to add a little more meat to the bones as we can also break these measures down into what we term the 3 levers of revenue transformation.

We can see them as levers simply because they are things we can control. We can pull these levers to change results. We might not be able to control much in the revenue process (despite people thinking the contrary), but these we can. Let's look at them in turn.

V #1: Value

We have been hardwired over the years to think about value in terms of how much value we bring to our buyers, and this is right. But in this case, we are discussing the value or price of what you sell. Or to be specific, our average sales price.

Of course, how much we can sell something is directly and indirectly related to how much value we can bring, so don't dismiss the idea of value in its other context. This is not rocket science. In its simplest terms, you make more money if you increase your selling price. But it's a great deal more than that, as increasing your sales price is compounding. And compounding is, according to Einstein, the world's eighth wonder. Actually, the full quote is, 'Compound interest is the eighth wonder of the world. He who understands it, earns it; he who doesn't, pays it', and there is no definitive evidence that he actually said or wrote it. But let's not spoil a good story with facts, as the statement is true.

Let's take an example. I have used small numbers to make it clear for everyone. But you can add your own numbers in if you like and see the impact for you. Here we go.

Let's say you have a service that is priced at £100 per 'unit', and you decide to increase the price by 2%. After the increase, the new selling price would be £102 per unit.

In the first year, let's assume you sell 100 units of the service. With the original price, your total revenue would have been £10,000 (100 units × £100 per unit). However, with the increased price, your total revenue becomes £10,200 (100 units × £102 per unit). The additional 2% increase in price has led to an extra £200 in revenue for the year.

Now, let's consider the compound impact over multiple years. Assuming a constant demand for your service, let's look at the revenue over a five-year period:

Year 1:
Original price: £10,000
Increased price: £10,200

Year 2:
Original price (assuming no change in demand): £10,000
Increased price: £10,404 (£10,200 × 102%)

Year 3:
Original price (assuming no change in demand): £10,000
Increased price: £10,612.08 (£10,404 × 102%)

Year 4:
Original price (assuming no change in demand): £10,000
Increased price: £10,824.32 (£10,612.08 × 102%)

Year 5:
Original price (assuming no change in demand): £10,000
Increased price: £11,040.96 (£10,824.32 × 102%)

As you can see, over the course of five years, the compound impact of a 2% increase in selling price each year has resulted in significantly higher revenues compared to the original price. The cumulative effect of the price increase compounds, leading to an increasing revenue stream over time.

And this is with small numbers. Add a few zeros to it and it becomes even more meaningful. Fun stuff! The challenge, of course, is how many of us are actually doing this. We are often highly reluctant to increase our selling prices by even a modest percentage as we fear our buyers will take a walk, but the evidence of that is not true. Far from being a problem, raising our average selling price can have a number of benefits, including these.

- **Increased profit margins:** The most obvious benefit is higher profit margins. Increasing your selling price while keeping your costs relatively stable will generate more revenue per sale, resulting in improved profitability. This extra profit can be reinvested in your business, which is a problem that often stagnates businesses.

- **Improved perceived value:** Raising your prices can positively influence buyers' perception of your product or service. A higher price often implies higher quality, exclusivity, or added value. A brilliant example of this is VW. They are the masters of rebranding essentially the same vehicle with different brands, to meet perceived value. Just don't tell Porsche, Audi, VM, Skoda, and Seat drivers they are driving the same vehicles, as they freak out!

- **Enhanced brand image:** Connecting with the above, increasing your prices can contribute to building a premium brand image. A higher price communicates exclusivity and can help position your business as a market leader. This can increase brand loyalty, trust, and a stronger market position. Cough, Apple, cough!

- **Support for growth and innovation:** As I mentioned in the first point, higher profit margins resulting from increased prices can provide your business with the financial resources needed for growth, innovation, and investment in research and development. This enables you to enhance your products, expand into new markets, invest in marketing efforts, or develop new offerings to stay ahead of the competition. This can allow you to create the differentiation you need, and the buyer is paying for it.

- **Better segmentation:** A price increase can help you segment your customer base. Some customers may be price-sensitive and opt for lower-priced alternatives, while others may perceive the increased price as a sign of enhanced quality or exclusivity and be willing to pay more. By targeting buyers willing to pay a premium, you can focus your efforts on higher-value segments and optimize your marketing and product strategies accordingly. Again, look to VW, who know how to do this well. They know Porsche drivers will pay more than necessary for the badge, and Skoda are more frugal. Many of the cars are the same underneath, but they are positioned differently. And guess which one brings the most profit!

- **Reduced dependency on volume:** This links to our next V, but increasing prices allow you to rely less on high sales volumes to achieve profitability. Instead of selling a large number of products or services, you can aim for fewer sales at higher price points, which may lead to reduced operational costs, lower inventory levels, and more efficient resource allocation. This can be hugely useful as a tool to impact performance.

Easy, right? Well, yeah, on paper, but the reality is there are a number of other tactics you can employ to raise your selling price. Here are some strategies to consider.

- **Enhance product quality:** Think about how you can improve the quality of your product by using higher-grade materials, enhancing durability, or adding new features that provide additional value to buyers. A superior product can justify a higher price point. Just remember that the increases in quality should be low cost to you but high value to the buyer.
- **Build brand reputation:** Invest in building a strong brand image and reputation. Focus on creating a perception of value, trust, and reliability associated with your brand. Like Porsche, a well-established brand often attracts higher prices due to loyalty and perceived quality.
- **Differentiate your product:** Find unique selling points or points of differentiation that set your product apart from competitors.

This could include innovative features, superior service, exclusive designs, or specialized customization options. By offering something distinct, buyers will be willing to pay a premium. Don't forget here that YOU are also the product, so think about how you differentiate. Differentiate around how you sell, how you create demand, and even how you price.

- **Provide a superior buyer experience:** Offer exceptional service and support. By providing personalized assistance, quick response times, and going above and beyond for buyers, you can justify charging a higher price due to your added value.
- **Bundle or upsell:** Offer complementary products or services as part of a package deal or upsell buyers to higher-priced variants or add-ons. You can increase the overall selling price by demonstrating the additional benefits buyers can gain from purchasing more. Simply increase the size of the pie!
- **Target premium market segments:** Identify and target niche or premium market segments that are willing to pay a premium for quality, exclusivity, or unique offerings. Tailor your marketing and product positioning to appeal to these specific groups. In other words, find another pie!
- **Offer financing or payment options:** Provide flexible financing or payment options such as instalment plans, leasing, or subscriptions. By breaking down the price into smaller, more manageable payments, buyers may be more willing to invest in a higher-priced product. Let's be super honest; the huge swing to things that are '… as a service', are just pricing plans in reality.

So that's lever number 1. What's next?

V #2: Volume

Just like value, volume is another lever we can play with. This one is interesting as, in some cases, it is directly related to value.

Volume also talks to the number of new selling opportunities in the top of the funnel. One of the arts of selling is to keep filling the funnel. This is where the symbiotic relationship between sales and marketing is essential. For example, it's the reason why companies often have a sale or run special offers. They drop the price to increase volume. Now this can be just to shift stock, but it's also there to impact the sales and even to buy entire markets as volume brings inertia.

We've all seen 'introductory offers' that are designed to get buyers first to create a buzz in the market. When you can increase volume and value, you have something very special, and the results are nothing short of exponential. If you don't believe me, look at each of Apple's iPhone launches.

Like value, increasing volume is obviously beneficial (just watch out that you can deliver on the volume!), but some other benefits might have passed you by.

- **Increased revenue:** Yep, let's start with the obvious one. Higher revenue is the most immediate benefit of increasing sales volume. Selling more units or securing more contracts generates higher overall income, contributing to your business's financial growth and stability.
- **Economies of scale:** Your business can use economies of scale as sales volume increases. This means that your average production and operational costs per unit may decrease due to factors such as bulk purchasing, improved efficiency, optimized logistics, and spreading fixed costs over a larger output. This can result in higher profit margins and improved competitiveness.
- **Enhanced market share:** Increasing sales volume often means gaining a larger market share. By capturing more of the market demand, you establish a stronger presence, potentially outperform competitors, and solidify your market position. A larger market share can lead to increased brand recognition, loyalty, and more growth opportunities. Inertia!

- **Improved negotiating power:** When your sales volume is higher, you may gain more leverage in negotiations with suppliers, vendors, and partners. The ability to purchase larger quantities can lead to favourable terms, discounts, or exclusive arrangements, ultimately reducing costs and improving profitability. As with value, we are changing the pie.

- **Enhanced brand awareness:** Increasing sales volume often involves reaching more buyers, which can result in heightened brand awareness. A broader base and increased visibility can help your business build a strong brand presence, attract new buyers through referrals or word-of-mouth, and create a positive reputation in the marketplace. And who wouldn't want that?

- **Better utilization of resources:** Vital for service organizations, increasing sales volume allows you to utilize your business's resources better. You can achieve higher output levels without significant cost increases by efficiently utilizing your workforce. This improves overall operational efficiency and resource allocation.

- **Potential for expansion:** Higher sales volume can provide the financial foundation for business expansion. The increased revenue and profitability can be reinvested in research and development, new product lines, geographic expansion, acquisitions, or market diversification. Expanding your business can open up new opportunities, increase market reach, and strengthen your competitive position.

So, a big tick for volume. But what might be some tactics to help us increase volume? There are no surprises here, but volume is a function of the whole revenue process. In fact, I would argue that this is where the benefits of a fully integrated revenue strategy, over a sales, marketing, and customer success function, really kick in.

I appreciate that not all of the tactics that follow will be applicable to you, but take what you need and file the rest, as you never know when you may need them in the future. Here we go:

- **Targeted marketing:** Identify your target audience and tailor your marketing efforts to reach them directly. Utilize all the various channels such as social media, email marketing, content marketing, and search engine optimization (SEO) to attract potential buyers. Sounds so obvious, but in my experience most people throw the spaghetti at the wall and wait to see what sticks, wasting time, energy, and reputation.

- **Buyer segmentation:** Divide your base into segments based on demographics, interests, buying behaviour, or other relevant factors. This enables you to create personalized marketing campaigns and offers that resonate with each segment. Just like targeted marketing, segmentation drives focus, which drives effectiveness, but it is only effective when you are brave enough to realize that not every buyer is a buyer. Learn this early and see your results improve and your customer acquisition costs (CAC; cost is the cost of winning a customer to purchase a product or service) fall.

- **Upselling and cross-selling:** A really simple one – used well by a few; ignored way too often. Encourage buyers to purchase additional products or upgrade their existing purchases. Offer complementary products or services during the buying process or recommend relevant items to increase the average order value.

- **Improve experience:** A tough one to crack, but when you do, this can be a highly effective strategy and differentiator. Focus on providing exceptional customer service at every touchpoint. Enhance your website's usability, streamline the checkout process, and promptly respond to buyer inquiries. Satisfied buyers are more likely to make repeat purchases and refer others. Remember fuel versus friction?

- **Referral programmes:** Encourage your existing buyers to refer their friends, family, or colleagues to your business by offering incentives like discounts, rewards, or exclusive access to certain features. This can expand your base through word-of-mouth marketing. I am still amazed at how few sellers do this, or at least do this well. It is by far the cheapest way to generate more business, and its one that is in our control as sellers (although it can be easily automated). I would bet that this is something every organization can improve on.

- **Strategic partnerships:** Collaborate with complementary businesses or influencers in your industry to leverage their customer base and expand your reach. This can involve co-marketing campaigns, joint ventures, or affiliate partnerships. Health warning here, though: Be careful who you hitch your wagon to. Make sure they share your values and vision so that you don't end up in conflict.

- **Enhance product visibility:** Optimize your product listings and descriptions to improve their visibility on search engines and e-commerce platforms. Utilize high-quality images, accurate product details, and buyer reviews to build trust and attract more potential buyers. This is where good enough is not good enough. Work every word, work every image. Know how to tag and understand the keywords that light up your buyers.

- **Retention:** Implement strategies to retain existing buyers, as it is often more cost-effective than acquiring new ones. Offer loyalty programs, personalized recommendations, or exclusive content to reward loyalty and encourage repeat purchases. There is often so much focus on what we are putting into the funnel, we forget to check what is leaking out. Check to see when, where, and why your buyers are not being retained.

- **Continuous improvement:** And finally, regularly analyse sales data, buyer feedback, and market trends to identify areas for improvement. Adjust your strategies accordingly, whether it's optimizing your product offerings, refining your pricing strategy, or updating your marketing campaigns. Make it part of the system and something you do regularly rather than something reactive when things have gone belly up. In good and bad times, the numbers are your friend!

Volume is a very powerful lever for us, and one that we are in more control of than any of the other two. Like I said at the beginning, combine improvements in value and volume, and you have another rocket ship. But there is one more lever to discuss: velocity.

V #3: Velocity

Say hello to a good friend of mine: velocity. I say 'a good friend' as this is where much of what we are talking about comes together. Before I get into that, let's define what velocity means.

Simply put, velocity is how quickly we can sell something.

If you consider value and volume, this multiplier shows how often you repeat the success. I often think about this as a cyclist thinks about their pedal stroke. Value and volume dictate the power of each stroke; velocity is how often that stroke happens. The great thing about velocity is that it can also provide us with both leading and lagging indicators, which means we can measure and adjust all the time.

Our lagging indicator here is the time to close. This simple measure counts how many days it takes for a sale to close end to end, from when we first saw it as a prospect to when we got a signed contract. As you can imagine, depending on your business, that may vary hugely from hours to years. There is no right answer here, but the global truth is, if you can make it shorter, that's good. You want to measure and see a downward trend in this number. We should be constantly asking ourselves how we can reduce the time to close.

Our leading indicator is the time in stage. Another simple metric measures how long it takes for a sale to progress through each step of the sales process. As previously, we want to reduce this number, but as this metric is granular, we can start to ask a more specific question: How can we reduce the time in this stage? Any changes made here will impact the overall time to close, but it gives you many more options. Simply, analysing each step will give you further insights into what you can do, and always remember that removing friction is more effective than adding fuel. Spotted a theme yet?

I've done it with the other two Vs, so for completeness, here is a list of some tactics you can use to improve your velocity.

- **Streamline your selling map:** Sorry to bang on about it, but it removes the friction. Evaluate your selling map and identify any bottlenecks or areas of inefficiency. Simplify and streamline the steps involved, minimizing unnecessary tasks and reducing friction. This can help accelerate the sales cycle and increase the overall velocity. Think of it like oiling the wheels.
- **Improve lead qualification:** Focus on targeting and qualifying high-quality leads more likely to convert into buyers. Refine your lead generation strategies and qualification criteria to ensure you spend your time and resources on the most promising opportunities. No more flying spaghetti monsters.
- **Implement sales enablement tools:** I find it hard to believe that you don't already, but if you still think spreadsheets are sufficient, utilize sales enablement tools such as your CRM, sales analytics, and sales acceleration platforms. Go in search of the metrics and the insights. You may need a guide (remember, no sherpas allowed), but get friendly with data.
- **Embrace sales automation:** You can get friendly with data, but you need to give automation a proper hug! Identify areas of your

sales process that can be automated, such as email marketing campaigns, lead nurturing, or proposal generation. Automating repetitive tasks can free up your sales team's time and enable them to focus on higher-value activities that drive sales velocity.

- **Focus on upselling and cross-selling:** I apologize for repeating myself here. Look for opportunities to increase the average deal size (value) and generate additional revenue from existing buyers. Encourage upselling and cross-selling by identifying complementary products or services that align with their needs. This can help accelerate revenue velocity as upsell and cross opportunities naturally close quicker due to the existing relationship.

- **Nurture relationships:** You've gotten friendly with data and hugged automation, but now it's time to get close to your buyers. Invest in building and nurturing strong relationships. Implement customer success programs, provide excellent service, and maintain regular communication to maximize customer satisfaction and encourage repeat business.

- **Analyse and iterate:** Yes, this again! Continuously monitor and analyse your sales performance metrics. Identify areas of improvement, experiment with different strategies, and iterate based on the insights you gather. Regularly review and refine your tactics to increase sales velocity.

Predictive analytics: From guesswork to precision

Now let's just talk AI for a second. Gone are the days when forecasting relied on hunches and crossed fingers. AI can now transform our predictive analytics into a discipline closer to meteorology than mysticism. Here are some examples.

- Algorithms can now parse buyer sentiment, email response patterns, and CRM activity to forecast outcomes weeks before deals enter the pipeline. Imagine knowing a £100k opportunity

has a 92% likelihood of stalling unless specific interventions occur – like receiving a weather alert for your sales funnel.
- Traditional dashboards highlight problems; AI systems propose solutions. If pipeline velocity dips, the system might cross-reference historical data to recommend tailored coaching or process adjustments. True DIA (Data → Insight → Action).

The golden rule? AI amplifies human judgement; it doesn't replace it. Be wary of any solution that promises to do it for you.

Also, where legacy systems treat teams as monolithic units, AI can enable personalized performance tracking at scale. Here are two potential examples.

- New hires might have a 4-hour lead response benchmark, while veterans are held to 20-minute standards – creating customized training pathways without manual oversight.
- Metrics adapt to territory complexity, product lifecycle stages, or macroeconomic factors. For example, a £50k deal in a recession-hit sector could carry double the weight in assessments, acknowledging the nuanced challenges sellers face.

Putting it all together

When put together, the 3 Vs are a very powerful way of looking at how we sell. Whether you are a seller, a demand generator, or a leader, knowing what you can impact, and knowing which levers you can pull, gives you control over the end result. It gives you flexibility: if one number is off, you can look to compensate with another. Like a graphic equalizer (if you are old enough to remember those), you are able to tune your revenue performance to meet your unique circumstances, situation, product, and market.

And there is something else. If you combine all these factors together, you can create a single number. You can target a number that is (albeit lagging) covering all of your revenue processes – a revenue performance indicator (RPI), if you like. Here is how you can calculate it (got your pen ready?):

RPI takes into account various factors, including the number of opportunities, the average deal size, the win rate, and the length of the sales cycle.

The formula for calculating RPI is:

RPI = Number of opportunities × Average deal value
(Win rate/Sales cycle length)

While we have already discussed these, let's break down the formula's components just to have 100% clarity for everyone.

- **Number of opportunities:** This refers to the total number of potential deals or sales opportunities in the pipeline. It typically represents the number of qualified leads or prospects the revenue team is actively working on.
- **Average deal value:** This means each closed deal's average monetary value. It helps determine the revenue impact of each individual sale.
- **Win rate:** The win rate represents the percentage of opportunities that result in a successful sale. It indicates the effectiveness of the sales team in converting leads into purchases.
- **Sales cycle length:** This is the average time it takes for an opportunity to move through the entire sales process, from initial contact to closed deals. It reflects the efficiency and speed of the revenue team in closing deals.

By calculating the RPI, you can assess the health and effectiveness of your revenue operations, end to end. It provides you with a quantitative measure of sales performance, helps identify areas for improvement, and allows for better sales forecasting and resource allocation. Not too bad for just one number, and nearly as powerful as 42! (Look up Douglas Adams if you are confused by that reference.)

The power of incremental change

Whenever we are given a dial to play with, the temptation is to give it a hard turn and try to turn it up, and this is true here. But there are a couple of things to consider:

1) These are compound multipliers. This means if we did a 5% change on each metric, it is more powerful than increasing one metric by 50%.
2) Small change done well is better than big change done badly. Focus on doing small incremental changes more than big bold changes. They will be more sustainable and will yield better long-term results.

The latter is a very well-known technique employed by sports coaches worldwide. They discovered that little and often, even as little as a few milliseconds in some sports, is the most effective way to improve overall improvement. Let me demonstrate this in a story. Well, two stories actually – as I will do one based on sport, then one focused on sales performance to make the point. Both are totally fictitious.

The power of incremental change in cycling: A tale of performance enhancement

Once upon a time, there was an aspiring cyclist called Sarah who dreamed of competing at the highest level. Sarah possessed raw talent and unwavering determination but struggled to reach her full potential. Recognizing the need for improvement, she focused on the power of incremental change.

Sarah began by focusing on her training routine. She implemented a systematic approach, gradually increasing the intensity and duration of her workouts. Sarah built endurance and stamina by consistently pushing herself a little further each day. Small, incremental changes to her training regimen resulted in significant improvements over time.

Next, Sarah turned her attention to her equipment. She worked closely with a knowledgeable cycling coach who helped her to optimize her bike setup. Sarah achieved a more efficient and comfortable riding position through careful adjustments, such as tweaking saddle height, handlebar position, and pedal cleat alignment. These small refinements reduced wind resistance and allowed her to generate more power with each pedal stroke.

Sarah also recognized the importance of nutrition and recovery. She began paying closer attention to her diet, ensuring she consumed the right macronutrients, and stayed hydrated. She incorporated regular rest days into her training schedule, allowing her body to recover and adapt to the stress of intense workouts. These incremental changes to her lifestyle helped to optimize her performance and minimize the risk of injury or burnout.

As Sarah continued her journey, she sought guidance from sports psychologists to fine-tune her mental approach. She learned to manage pre-race nerves, maintain focus during challenging moments, and develop a positive mindset. Through daily visualization exercises and affirmation techniques, she harnessed the power of her mind to drive her performance to new heights.

With each race, Sarah analyzed her performance and identified areas for further improvement. She noticed her weaknesses and sought ways to turn them into strengths. It could be slightly adjusting her cornering technique, refining her sprinting form, or enhancing her climbing ability. Sarah knew that even the smallest tweaks, when accumulated, could lead to significant gains.

Over time, Sarah's commitment to incremental change paid off. She began achieving personal bests, climbing up the ranks in races, and catching the attention of professional cycling teams. Her consistent pursuit of improvement, one small step at a time, transformed her into a formidable competitor.

You get the point, right? Little and often and across multiple factors – it gets exponential results.

Let's go again, but let's be overtly focused on a seller so there can be no confusion in metaphor.

The power of incremental change in sales performance: Pedalling towards success

Once upon a time, there was a seller called Gerry who was passionate about their job but struggled to meet their targets consistently. Determined to turn things around, they realized they needed to embrace the power of incremental change to boost their performance.

Gerry began by honing their communication and interpersonal skills. They sought out training programmes, attended workshops, and read books on effective selling techniques. Through continuous learning and practice, Gerry refined their ability to listen actively, build rapport with clients, and deliver persuasive presentations. These incremental improvements in their communication skills allowed them to connect better with prospects and foster stronger relationships.

Recognizing the importance of product knowledge, Gerry dedicated daily time to studying their company's offerings. They immersed themselves in the features, benefits, and competitive advantages of the products they sold. By deepening their understanding and articulating the value proposition clearly, Gerry instilled confidence in their prospects and positioned themselves as a trusted advisor. The incremental change in their product knowledge resulted in increased credibility and higher conversion rates.

Gerry also realized the significance of effective time management in selling. They identified areas where they were wasting valuable time and made small adjustments to their daily routine. They prioritized their activities, eliminated unnecessary tasks, and created a structured schedule that allowed them to focus on high-value activities, such as prospecting and following up with leads. These incremental changes in time management boosted their productivity and ensured they consistently engaged in revenue-generating activities.

To further enhance their performance, Gerry utilized technology to their advantage. They embraced the CRM to organize and track their sales activities. With a clear overview of their prospects and their interactions, they were able to follow up timely, personalize their approach, and nurture leads effectively. By leveraging technology, Gerry experienced incremental improvements in their efficiency and effectiveness as a selling professional.

In addition to personal development, Gerry recognized the importance of collaboration. They actively sought feedback from their colleagues and managers, participating in meetings and sharing best practices. By embracing a culture of learning and collaboration, Gerry gained valuable insights, refined their strategies, and adapted their approach based on the collective wisdom of their team. These incremental changes in collaboration and knowledge sharing elevated their performance.

Over time, Gerry's commitment to incremental change paid off. They began consistently meeting and exceeding their targets, earning recognition within the organization, and increasing their commission earnings. Gerry transformed into a top-performing seller by embracing small, continuous improvements in their skills, knowledge, time management, and collaboration.

Okay, so story time is over, and I am sure you get where I am going with this. It's about regularly doing little things well, over several areas, and avoiding the temptation to go mad in one specific area. If there is one thing you take from this book, let it be this, as this should be taught in schools as a core principle in life, as it can be applied to literally anything, from money to relationships.

Measure beyond the number

But there is more to consider. If we just measure selling performance by the KPIs, we are missing a vital piece of the puzzle.

We need to go beyond traditional metrics and consider the measurement of mental fitness and well-being. We need to look at the person as a whole human, not just a machine that churns results. Evaluating mental fitness and well-being alongside traditional metrics offers a more comprehensive understanding of our performance and supports our overall success and well-being.

As discussed in the earlier chapter, mental fitness plays a significant role in our selling performance as the revenue process means we face intense pressure, rejection, and demanding targets daily. The ability to handle stress, maintain focus, and stay motivated is crucial for sustained high performance. By measuring mental fitness, organizations can identify potential issues or areas of improvement, provide the necessary support, and enhance their teams' overall resilience and performance.

Measuring well-being is also essential for all our employee satisfaction and long-term success. Selling can be an especially emotionally challenging profession, and neglecting well-being can lead to burnout, decreased motivation, and higher turnover rates. Assessing well-being factors such as work–life balance, job satisfaction, and overall happiness helps organizations to gauge the health of their sales team and identify strategies to improve morale, productivity, and retention. And let's not forget that retention is the #1 challenge for global businesses worldwide today.

When employees feel that their mental health and well-being are valued, they are likelier to thrive, be engaged, and achieve their full potential. It encourages open communication, reduces mental health stigma, and promotes a supportive environment where individuals can seek help when needed. Prioritizing mental fitness and well-being contributes to a positive work culture that values its employees' holistic success and happiness.

Traditional metrics like the ones discussed earlier (e.g., revenue, pipeline, conversion rates, etc.) primarily focus on outcomes, neglecting the human element. By integrating mental fitness and well-being measures, organizations gain insights into the underlying factors influencing sales performance. This holistic view enables targeted interventions and mentoring that address both the tangible metrics and the psychological factors that impact performance.

Let's also not forget that measuring mental fitness and well-being aligns with the growing recognition of the importance of mental health in overall wellness. As society becomes more aware of the significance of mental well-being, organizations that proactively address these factors gain a competitive advantage in attracting and retaining top talent. Sales professionals are more likely to be attracted to organizations that prioritize their mental health needs and provide a supportive work environment.

Our CRMs are really bad at measuring these things, which means we need to put some effort into measuring well-being in other ways, but programmes like Positive Intelligence (www.positiveintelligence.com) are capable and, when brought together with sales metrics, start to paint a true, multi-dimensional view of our revenue teams.

This can truly be a competitive advantage, as well as being the right thing to do.

In summary, remember there is always a balance between leading and lagging indicators, but if you are focused on the 3 Vs (value, volume, and velocity), your pencil will remain sharp and help you to think about the RPI (Revenue Performance Indicator).

If you want a one-pager to help you remember these important terms, just visit https://infinite.mentorgroup.co.uk/tools, where you can download the 3 Vs cheat sheet.

Well, we are nearly there now, team; thanks for sticking with me so far. There's one last thing to get into, and that's revenue realization.

Chapter 16

Revenue realization

I do need to be careful with my terms here, as revenue realization can be confused with revenue recognition, and that's a whole other thing.

Revenue recognition is the process of recording and reporting revenue in a company's financial statements. It involves recognizing revenue when it is earned and determining the appropriate timing and amount to be recorded.

The concept of revenue recognition is based on the Generally Accepted Accounting Principles (GAAP) and International Financial Reporting Standards (IFRS). According to these standards, revenue should be recognized when the following criteria are met.

- **Revenue is earned:** The goods or services have been delivered to the buyer, and the company has fulfilled its obligations under the terms of the sale or contract.
- **Revenue is measurable:** The amount of revenue can be reliably measured, usually in monetary terms. This requires the company to have a reasonable estimate of the consideration it expects to receive.
- **Revenue is collectable:** There is a reasonable assurance that the company will collect the payment for the goods or services rendered.

But revenue realization is something different: it is the sum of the parts of the entire Infinite Selling concept. It is the purpose of the Infinite Loop. It is the purpose of the dance we do with our buyers.

Ultimately, nothing else really matters. If demand generation doesn't end up as realized revenue, there was no point in doing it. If the negotiation training that we put everybody on didn't move the revenue needle, that too wasn't worth the investment.

Revenue realization reigns supreme.

Sounds super simple, right? And it is – but ultimately, we all get this wrong. And this, again, comes down to what we discussed earlier, and what we measure. Remember: what we measure gets done. It's such a cliché, but it is also so accurate. And this brings me to the concept we have already discussed briefly – EQ, IQ, and XQ – and it's worth going deeper here.

The only conversation that matters

We'd better get started by making sure we all understand the basic concepts of EQ, IQ, and XQ. Well, actually, let's start with EQ and IQ. These are two different types of intelligence that are often discussed in the context of human capabilities.

IQ, or intelligence quotient, measures a person's cognitive abilities, particularly their intellectual capacity and problem-solving skills. It is typically assessed through standardized tests that measure skills such as logical reasoning, mathematical aptitude, language comprehension, and spatial awareness. IQ is often associated with academic intelligence and has traditionally been used to measure a person's intellectual potential.

In revenue realization, IQ can be seen in the following.

- **Logical reasoning:** Team members with strong logical reasoning skills can effectively analyse buyer needs, identify patterns, and logically connect buyer requirements and product offerings. This helps them to tailor their selling approach and present persuasive arguments to potential clients.

- **Problem solving:** We all encounter various challenges and obstacles during the sales process. A high IQ enables individuals to think critically, creatively, and analytically when addressing buyer concerns, objections, or complex selling situations. They can devise innovative solutions and adapt their strategies to meet buyers' needs effectively.

- **Learning agility:** The act of selling is an ever-evolving field, and the most successful team members continuously learn and adapt to new products, market trends, and buyer preferences. Higher IQ individuals often exhibit strong learning agility, enabling them to quickly grasp new information, absorb training materials, and stay ahead.

But how many of us know people with a brain the size of a planet who can't even open a front door? IQ is, therefore, just one part of the story. And this is where EQ comes in.

The concept of emotional intelligence gained significant attention through the work of psychologist Daniel Goleman, who popularized the term in his 1995 book, *Emotional Intelligence: Why It Can Matter More Than IQ*. Goleman's research highlighted the importance of emotional intelligence in personal and professional success, and he coined the phrase EQ.

EQ, or emotional quotient, refers to a person's emotional intelligence. It is the ability to recognize, understand, manage, and use emotions effectively in various social and interpersonal contexts. Emotional intelligence includes empathy, self-awareness, self-regulation, social awareness, and relationship management skills. EQ relates to how individuals perceive and manage their emotions, and navigate and interact with others in social situations.

While IQ focuses on cognitive abilities and problem-solving skills, EQ emphasizes emotional awareness and interpersonal skills. Both IQ and EQ contribute to a person's overall intelligence and can influence their success and well-being in different areas of life, including personal relationships, career, and overall mental health.

In revenue realization, EQ can be seen in the following.

- **Empathy:** Team members with high EQ can empathize with their buyers, understanding their needs, concerns, and emotions. They actively listen, show genuine interest, and tailor their approach to address buyer pain points. This empathy helps build rapport and trust, leading to stronger relationships and increased revenue success.
- **Relationship building:** EQ enables team members to establish and maintain strong relationships with the company's buyers, partners, and others. They can read social cues, adapt their communication style, and build rapport with individuals from diverse backgrounds. Team members with high EQ can establish connections based on trust, mutual understanding, and long-term value, fostering loyalty and repeat business.
- **Self-motivation:** Team members with high EQ can stay motivated, maintain a positive mindset, and bounce back from setbacks (the true definition of mental fitness). They can set goals, stay focused, and keep a drive to achieve results despite challenges.

The bottom line is that people with a balanced combination of both IQ and EQ tend to excel in their roles.

But what about XQ?

XQ, or execution quotient – sometimes referred to as execution intelligence – encompasses a set of skills and attributes that enable individuals to translate ideas, plans, or strategies into action and achieve desired outcomes. It involves qualities such as goal orientation, organizational skills, attention to detail, adaptability, resilience, decision-making, and the ability to drive projects to completion.

XQ is particularly relevant in revenue and leadership contexts, as it emphasizes the practical application of knowledge and the ability to execute plans and initiatives. It's the 'So, what are we going to do?' skill.

It focuses on the implementation phase and the actual delivery of results rather than just conceptual thinking or emotional intelligence.

While XQ may not be as widely discussed or measured as IQ or EQ, the concept highlights the importance of effective execution and follow-through in achieving success in various endeavours – including business, projects, and personal goals. It's no good if you have all the intelligence and all the emotions but can't actually deliver anything!

In revenue realization, XQ can be seen in the following.

- **Goal orientation:** Team members with a high XQ focus on setting and achieving their goals. They clearly understand their targets, develop action plans, and work diligently to meet or exceed their objectives. They demonstrate a strong drive and determination to execute their sales strategies effectively. They know where they are going and have a plan to get there.

- **Organization and time management:** XQ involves effectively managing time and resources. Team members with a high XQ prioritize their tasks, allocate time efficiently, and stay organized. They use tools and systems to streamline processes, track interactions, and to ensure they execute well-structured activities.

- **Adaptability and flexibility:** Revenue generation, as we all know, requires adapting to changing circumstances. Buyers do have a habit of throwing us curve balls, and we need to be able to catch them. Team members with a high XQ are likely to be more adaptable and flexible in their approach. They can quickly adjust their strategies based on the buyer's feedback, market trends, or unexpected challenges. Their agility allows them to respond effectively to different situations and execute alternative approaches when necessary.

- **Resilience and perseverance:** Our world can be challenging and involve facing rejection or encountering setbacks. Team members with a high XQ demonstrate resilience and perseverance in the face of adversity. They bounce back from rejection, learn from failures, and maintain a positive attitude to keep moving forward and executing their sales strategies. We've discussed this before when we looked at mental fitness, and there is an argument to say that this could fit into an entirely separate 'q'.

- **Cadence:** Cadence generally refers to a rhythmic or patterned sequence, and whether used in speech, fitness (especially cycling), or music, doing something regularly enhances the experience, efficiency, communication, and coordination. Where we are using our XQ, and we are operating in a repeated pattern, we are developing the muscle memory that drives superior performance as a seller, and a reassuringly familiar experience for the buyer, reducing friction.

As mentioned before, Daniel Goleman evidenced that the most successful people were those with a good balance of EQ and IQ. What I am suggesting is that without XQ, the EQ and the IQ don't really matter, as nothing actually gets done.

We must put our hands to the pump and do something with the other two skills. XQ is the secret sauce and, in many ways, is the multiplier and a compensator. When balanced with IQ and EQ, XQ can significantly multiply our results. You could almost rephrase the equation:

$IQ + EQ \times XQ = success,$

or $(IQ + EQ) \times XQ = S$ (if you want to get nerdy).

But XQ can also compensate when IQ or EQ is not in balance. You may not get the explosive results you could get when all are in balance, but good execution can cover a multitude of sins – but only for a time.

An old colleague of mine wasn't blessed with great IQ but, as an ex-soldier, he knew how to get things done. He had strong XQ. In fact, he was very pleased with his reputation for his ability to 'run through walls until told to stop'.

Sure, he was a blunt instrument, but that's better than being a brain on a stick with no one to talk to, or an empath who is too busy knitting yoghurt to have a productive meeting with a buyer.

In the last chapter, we explored the one number to rule them all as your indicator of revenue success, and now I would say that the one conversation to rule them all, when it comes to enablement, is whether it will improve their EQ, IQ, and XQ. If it's not impacting one of those areas, or there is an imbalance in the three areas, it's worth considering whether it's worth doing or whether a course correction is required.

Now, while we are talking about these three intelligences, it would be remiss to discuss the fourth intelligence, Artificial Intelligence.

AI's role in Infinite Selling isn't about replacing the human nuance. Instead, we should be thinking about we can use it to elevate our EQ, IQ, and XQ to levels that redefine efficiency and deliver insight.

EQ: The emotional amplifier

Those familiar with me know that I struggle with empathy. Whether this is due to being on the spectrum or because I am a sociopath is for you to decide. However, wouldn't it be fascinating if an empathy advisor could whisper real-time insights about your buyer's unspoken hesitations? I know I could certainly use that on date night!

AI may not be capable of feeling emotions, but it excels at decoding them through vocal cadence, word choice, and even strategic silences. Take a look at these examples.

- **Sentiment mapping:** During negotiations, AI can flag subtle tonal shifts – polite agreement masking uncertainty – prompting you to pivot from feature-pushing to addressing hidden concerns.

- **Empathy scaffolding:** Struggling to relate to a niche challenge? AI cross-references historical interactions, suggesting language that mirrors the buyer's industry pain points. Useful.

Critically, AI will never replace empathy, but it can structure it. Think of it as training wheels for newer team members or a mental subroutine for veterans to validate instincts.

IQ: The data whisperer

If IQ is the engine, AI is the turbocharger (told you I like turbos) – processing information at speeds that leave spreadsheets in the dust. Here are a few examples.

- **Pattern recognition:** AI can mine CRM data, email threads, and deal histories to spotlight trends invisible to the naked eye. Did 73% of stalled deals falter at the same contractual clause? The algorithm spots it mid-conversation.
- **Learning accelerants:** Remember that two-hour webinar on value-based selling? AI can distil it into a five-minute cheat sheet infused with examples from your active pipeline. (This point is particularly interesting to Matt and me, as that has, of course, been our traditional bread and butter. However, times are changing, and we need to adapt as well.)

The brilliance lies in AI handling the IQ heavy lifting – data crunching, trend spotting, knowledge recall – freeing us for strategic thinking. It's cognitive bandwidth expansion, not replacement.

XQ: The execution multiplier

Many parts of XQ thrive on precision, and here, AI operates like a Swiss Army knife for productivity. From personal experience, AI has radically changed how I work and significantly improved my productivity. As before, a couple of examples follow.

- **Predictive prioritization:** AI can analyse our calendars, deal stages, and buyer responsiveness to auto-schedule tasks. Prep for negotiation or chase a lukewarm lead? The system can nudge decisively. Maybe even learn from its mistakes, which is more than I ever do.
- **Adaptive playbooks:** Static sales guides and enablement materials often gather dust. AI-powered playbooks evolve. Lose a deal over implementation timelines? The system could auto-update future scenarios with pre-emptive FAQs.

The hidden gem? Cadence reinforcement. AI doesn't have to be relegated to just remind you to follow up – it can also analyse how to follow up. Did the buyer respond best to succinct morning emails with bullet-pointed ROI? The system logs it, replicates it, and trains you (that's a reversal of normal roles) to refine execution rhythms. Ultimately, the good news is that we can impact our EQ, IQ, and XQ, but this often requires some external help. And this brings me nicely to the next topic: coaching.

Death to coaching

I will probably upset a few people in this discussion. My views may be unpopular with some, but please keep an open mind, as while I titled this 'Death to coaching', it has a place, and an important one at that.

So, what is coaching? Why is it so popular?

As most good things did, it started with the Greeks, who believed that physical fitness was a vital part of society. These wise Greeks saw the potential in their less-than-athletic brethren and decided to lend a helping hand. They provided guidance, encouragement, and a fair amount of shouting to help these poor souls become slightly less terrible at sports.

Fast forward a few centuries and coaching had become common in various sports. Coaches became an integral part of the sports world, whether it was the frenzied cries of a football coach on the sidelines, or the calm instructions whispered in a gymnast's ear. They were the cheerleaders, motivators, and tactical geniuses who helped athletes unlock their true potential.

What is truly interesting, however, is that they were not all very good at the topic they were coaching. They were not all excellent football players or gymnasts or whatever; they were good at unlocking potential.

But as time went on, people started to realize that the coaching principles weren't limited to just sports. Enter the world of business coaching, where executives and entrepreneurs sought guidance in navigating the treacherous waters of corporate success. We have all been there – a stuffy boardroom filled with stressed-out executives, their ties pulled uncomfortably tight around their necks. In walks a business coach armed with a PowerPoint presentation and an unyielding belief in the power of positive thinking. Suddenly, the room is filled with energy and optimism as this coach imparts wisdom, helps set goals, and shows them how to tap into their inner rock star (figuratively and sometimes literally).

The concept of coaching soon extended beyond the business realm and found its way into personal development and performance coaching. People from all walks of life sought guidance from these modern-day gurus to enhance their skills, boost their confidence, and achieve their dreams. It was as if coaches had become the fairy godmothers of the real world, helping Cinderella find her glass slipper or teaching Jack how to climb that beanstalk properly.

As I mentioned before, coaching has now evolved into a multi-billion-dollar industry with a vast array of specialities. You can find coaches for just about anything you can imagine: life coaches, wellness coaches, dating coaches, and even coaches who claim to be able to teach you how to speak to dolphins (although, let's be honest, that one might be a bit questionable).

The general principle, however, is that coaches don't tell you what to do; they help you find your own answers. They don't give opinions or advice; they just ask questions that extract your own answers. Remember this, as it is pivotal to why coaching in revenue teams needs to change.

This principle of staying neutral was popularized by the work of John Whitmore (a pioneer of executive coaching) and his GROW model.

The GROW model is a framework – a step-by-step guide for coaching. It stands for Goal, Reality, Options, and Way Forward. Each step is like a piece of the coaching puzzle, helping both the coach and the client navigate their way to success.

G is for 'Goal'. This is where you and your client start by setting a clear goal. Think of it as the destination you want to reach. It could be anything from smashing a presentation to conquering a fear of spiders. The key is to make it specific and measurable, like saying, 'I want to deliver a killer presentation that impresses my boss and colleagues.'

R is for 'Reality'. Once the goal is set, it's time to assess the current reality. It's like taking a snapshot of where things stand right now. You and your client explore their strengths, weaknesses, and the obstacles they may face. It's an honest and sometimes eye-opening conversation that helps you both understand the starting point.

O is for 'Options'. Now comes the fun part – brainstorming all the possible ways to reach that goal. It's like opening a treasure chest of ideas. You and your client explore different strategies, approaches, and alternatives. The more options, the merrier! It's a creative process that encourages out-of-the-box thinking and sparks new ideas.

W is for 'Way Forward'. After exploring the options, it's time to choose a path and create an action plan. You and your client decide on the best way to move forward. It's like charting a course on a map with milestones and steps. You break down the plan into manageable chunks, making tracking progress and staying motivated easier.

As you can imagine, it doesn't take a huge leap for someone to think, 'Well, if it's good enough for business performance in general, let's try it with our sellers.'

And it worked, but to a point.

What also happened during this time was that organizations started investing in training programmes that emphasized coaching skills. I know, as I have built a good number of them.

Sales managers were taught how to guide, support, and empower their selling teams to reach their full potential. This shift in focus, from a purely managerial role to that of a coach, allowed managers to take a more proactive and personalized approach to developing their team members.

But herein lies the problem. It is not that coaching or the principles of coaching are wrong; it's just that we are asking the wrong people to do it.

Revenue leaders, by their nature, are not natural coaches. They are skilled at many things but, in my experience, letting go and not giving their opinion or advice (remember my earlier point in one of my meanderings) is not one of them.

In theory, if we reposition the sales leadership role as a coach, everyone will see the benefit, and the sellers will benefit from the time spent with their leadership.

This is great in theory. Just one problem: leaders hate it!

On paper, 'leaders as coaches' is perfect. It solves many problems that are endemic in revenue leadership. From pipeline management to 'ride along' calls, coaching is the perfect vehicle for delivering support that was previously reserved for the higher echelons.

To be fair, we have seen some success with the model, and results, when done right, have exceeded our expectations. We have seen all the key metrics – volume, value, and velocity (the 3Vs) – improve with the correct implementation of coaching, and the ROI of the programme has been impressive; so impressive that it made us overlook one key area: how engaged the leaders actually were in coaching.

When we looked at the detail, we found that only about 20% of the sales leaders were coaching. The other 80% were either not coaching at all, only coaching sometimes, or worse, demeaning coaching as an effective part of sales leadership.

Digging in deeper, we could see what was really happening was that leaders hated the term 'coach' and did not want to be associated with it or what it stood for.

When you step back and think about it, you can see why. Coaching purists will tell you that a true coach doesn't know the answer and doesn't even need to know the context of the challenge being presented. Their job is to ask you questions that allow you to answer the questions yourself.

Now, given that leaders tend (and this is a stereotype) to have type A personalities (search for type A and B personalities online if you are not sure what these are), listening and suggesting are not one of their greatest strengths. It would not be too strong to say they actively looked down on that sort of behaviour. What is even more surprising is despite the evidence that the approach significantly improves performance, they were not interested.

Ultimately, this all comes down to ego. Leaders don't want to be seen as coaches. They want to be seen as leaders (don't even get me started on that comment!). So, it got us thinking, how can we achieve both?

What has come out of this is a subtle language change. It's a move away from coaching to mentoring. Mentoring has a very different connotation from coaching. Coaching can be seen as a softer skill. You mentor, however, when you are at the top of your field to those who need your support. It feeds the ego for sure, but it is, actually, in the context of revenue leadership, even more impactful on performance.

Sure, there is a fine line between mentoring and simply telling people what to do, but it's a middle ground – not soft and fluffy like coaching, but not as hard-edged and cutting as a dictatorship. Mentoring, we have found, hits the spot directly and allows sellers to benefit from leaders that have experience, making sure leaders are involved and engaged.

It's a win–win–win. The sellers win, the leader wins, and the company wins.

If we want to have coaches in the business, fine, but let them be dedicated resources that specialize in coaching and not as part of another role where it doesn't really fit. Instead, leaders should be empowered to act as mentors – a role that naturally aligns with their experience and character. By doing so, they unlock the full value of the insights, lessons, and wisdom they've gained on their journey to leadership. I know this may be seen as a picky bit of language, but it's a really important distinction and one that can really give an organization an edge.

Coaching and mentoring should be seen as two sides of the same coin.

When it comes to coaching, the focus is on helping individuals identify their goals, develop new skills, and find their own solutions. Coaches ask thought-provoking questions, challenge limiting beliefs, and provide guidance to support personal and professional growth. It's like having a cheerleader who empowers you to reach your full potential.

On the other hand, mentoring is like having a wise and experienced friend who shares their knowledge, insights, and experiences to help you along the way. As I said, mentors are typically more experienced individuals who offer advice, guidance, and wisdom based on their own journey. They provide valuable industry insights, share lessons learned, and may even open doors to new opportunities.

Coaching focuses more on the present and future, helping individuals set goals, overcome obstacles, and develop specific skills. Conversely, mentoring often involves a longer-term relationship and is more focused on sharing wisdom and experience gained over time.

We need to let the leaders do what they do best and have the space to lead and help them become better mentors.

The MENTOR model

Mentoring, like coaching, is a skill that can be learned, but while coaching usually follows a structured process, with defined sessions, goal setting, and specific action plans, mentoring, on the other hand, is often more informal and flexible, allowing for organic discussions and guidance based on the mentee's needs.

Having said that, there are some frameworks that we can use to help guide our leaders become better, including one conveniently called MENTOR. Let's take a look at it.

- **M** **Establish mutual expectations:** Start by clarifying and aligning expectations with your mentee. Discuss the goals, objectives, and boundaries of the mentoring relationship. This sets the foundation for a productive and meaningful mentoring journey. This resembles the G in GROW.
- **E** **Engage and encourage:** Create a supportive and open environment for your mentee. Listen actively, show empathy, and provide encouragement. Help them identify their strengths, passions, and areas for growth. Be a positive cheerleader, offering words of motivation and inspiration. This is probably the area that may need the most attention as often we find leaders lack real listing skills and are more likely to give opinions without listening to the problem.
- **N** **Navigate and nurture:** Guide your mentee through their journey by providing direction and insights. Share your knowledge, experiences, and lessons learned. Help them navigate challenges, make informed decisions, and set realistic goals. Nurture their growth by offering constructive feedback and gentle guidance. This is like O in GROW, but rather than

leaving all the options to the coachee, the mentor has the ability to add their own sprinkles (and who doesn't like sprinkles).

T **Transfer knowledge and skills:** Share your expertise, wisdom, and industry-specific knowledge. Provide resources, articles, or books that can help your mentee broaden their understanding. Offer practical advice and tools to develop specific skills. Transfer your knowledge to empower them on their path. This is the biggest difference between coaching and mentoring and is the biggest area of opportunity to make a real difference to our sellers.

O **Open doors and opportunities:** As a mentor, you can open doors and create opportunities for your mentee. Introduce them to your network, connect them with relevant contacts, or recommend them for projects or positions. Help expand their horizons and expose them to new possibilities. I have been fortunate enough to have had a couple of mentors in my time, and I would not be where I am now if it wasn't for the doors they opened and the opportunities they gave me.

R **Reflect and review:** Encourage regular reflection and review sessions with your mentee. Take time to assess progress, discuss challenges, and celebrate successes. Provide constructive feedback and help them identify areas for improvement. Reflect on the mentorship journey together and adjust as needed. This is another important distinction between coaching and mentoring, as coaching frameworks don't look at specific feedback. They rely on the conversation after the feedback has been given.

You can download a MENTOR cheat sheet if you visit https://infinite.mentorgroup.co.uk/tools.

Like I said, coaching isn't wrong, and it very much has a place, but in our context, mentoring is rules supreme and needs to take its place at the top table. We celebrate leaders' valuable contributions rather than relegating them to just asking (albeit great) questions.

And now to my final point, how do we know when we have arrived and are truly an Infinite seller? The answer is surprisingly simple.

Ease and flow

It may be surprisingly simple, making it even more curious as to why more people don't recognize its importance. As subjective as it may be, for the Infinite seller, the concept of 'ease and flow' is our final measure of success.

It's the one that tells us whether we are on track or off track and at the highest possible level. It transcends lead and lag measures and gives us our true north.

For many, this concept is so alien it's hard to comprehend, but let me try to give you a basic understanding of what I am extolling here, and please bear with me. If you can grasp this, it may just be the best thing you learn – not just in our mission of revenue realization but in life in general – as ease and flow is a general concept that can be applied to every area of your life, from your finances to your relationships.

Imagine you're at your desk, and everything feels smooth and effortless. There appears to be no friction at all. You're fully engaged in your tasks, and the ideas and solutions seem to flow effortlessly. You're in a state of ease, where work doesn't feel like a burden but rather an enjoyable and fulfilling experience.

It's the sort of feeling you get when you are doing something that you really like or interests you. It feels like the times you spend with your friends and family, where time whizzes by and the conversation flows without strain. It's almost like we are in a vacuum where there is this intense focus and calm, and our mind is clear.

Having this clear mind means that you're free from mental clutter and distractions and you can focus on the task at hand without being overwhelmed by annoying thoughts or worries. This clarity allows you to see the bigger picture and make informed decisions. When your mind is clear, you're also more creative and innovative. You can think outside the box, generate fresh ideas, and approach challenges from different angles. Stress or anxiety does not cloud your thoughts, enabling you to develop effective solutions.

Personally, I have generated my best ideas and thinking when my mind has been in neutral – like when I am out running in the morning or taking a shower. In this state of ease and clarity, you can enter a flow state.

'Flow' is a psychological term coined by psychologist Mihaly Csikszentmihalyi, which refers to a state of deep focus and immersion in an activity. Work becomes effortless when you're in flow, and time seems to fly by. You're fully absorbed and engaged in what you're doing.

I first experienced this when I learnt how to code. I would get to my desk and lose hours solving a problem. It generated unhealthy habits as well, though, like forgetting to eat, but my productivity skyrocketed.

Being in a state of flow at work has numerous benefits.

For example, as I just mentioned, it can enhance your productivity. You can accomplish tasks efficiently and effectively when you're in the flow, as your concentration is heightened and you can maintain a high level of performance and solve problems more easily.

Being in a state of ease and flow can also foster a positive work environment (bear with me on this, as I can sense your scepticism from here), as your enthusiasm and passion for your work can be contagious.

It can inspire and motivate others around you and can also improve collaboration and teamwork as you're more receptive to ideas and open to feedback. I know that sounds a little far-fetched, but think about it: Who do you enjoy working with the most? The person who doesn't want to be there or the passionate person? We may have empathy with the former, but the latter is the motivator.

And then, once in flow, the outcomes happen. They seem to arise naturally. They can just pop. And this is where we need to pay attention.

Recognizing what gets us to a place of ease and flow helps us to be able to create those circumstances so we can generate more of the same. This can be as simple as recognizing that we are more creative in the mornings, so then scheduling creative tasks first thing and leaving the dull administrative tasks until later in the day. Or vice versa if you prefer admin over creativity. No judgement here. We just need to learn what works. But then there is more.

When we talk about ease and flow, I have been coaching it in terms of what we like, and painting a picture that our lives can be filled with little fluffy clouds, with magical unicorns skipping across them. That's not my reality. My reality is that there are challenges every day. There are people I would prefer to avoid. There are times when I just want someone else to do it for me so that I can stay in bed.

The trick, though, is not to avoid these challenges. It's about being okay with the challenges and using ease and flow as the barometer for the solution and whether it is right.

Many people have written extensively on the dangers of trusting our feelings, and they are right to do so. Our feelings are often all over the place; the right choice one day is wrong the day after. Ease and flow are different, and it's tangible when it happens.

Let me give you an example I am sure you will all recognize: the coin flip. You flip a coin to decide on something you are unsure of, and when the coin lands, you immediately know if it was the right choice. There is something inside us that 'just knows'. That's ease and flow.

So, in revenue realization, this is the art of knowing what is right when we are looking to solve our buyer's challenges. It's about knowing the right thing to do as a leader. It can govern how we negotiate, what CRM to choose, what revenue generation campaign to work on, and even how we approach a face-to-face meeting with our buyers (strange, I know, but apparently, these do still happen occasionally despite the dominance of virtual meetings).

When we look at our part in the Infinite Selling process, we should always be checking in with ourselves to see whether we are in ease and flow. Anywhere we are not should be a yellow flag and something to explore.

Right at the beginning of the book, I explained how Infinite Selling is supposed to be a dance – a beautiful and effortless motion between us and our buyers. An elegant flow, ease and flow.

If I were to summarize this chapter, it would simply be to think about your XQ in your work (you can do it at home too if you like, but again, that's a different book).

Given that you have come this far in the book, I would suggest you already have EQ and IQ, and probably a good dose of XQ, but the intentional focus on XQ will bring you dividends and productivity that will take you to a whole other level.

I would also suggest that you look carefully at how you view coaching. If you are a leader, are you really coaching? If you are a seller, are you really being coached? Mentoring and the MENTOR model (remember, you can download the MENTOR cheat sheet by visiting our bonuses site at https://infinite.mentorgroup.co.uk/tools) can give you another perspective that may better suit you or your teams to drive revenue performance. But most of all, remember the ultimate litmus test: ease and flow.

Conclusion: The new world of revenue realization

As we close this book, I hope you can see the need to change from the old ways and methods, and the benefits we can achieve when we embrace the Infinite way. The world has changed so much in the last decade alone, I can only begin to imagine how it will change again, but at least you will have a strong foundation to build upon.

As emphasized earlier in the book, sellers need to catch up with the buyers. They are moving fast, and their expectations of us are changing daily. Sticking to old, stale methodologies will only push us further away from our lifeblood, and while the old seller's personality and skills are dying, we need to step up and adapt.

I am sure some of you will be contemplating how you will fit into this new world, and some will even think that selling is no longer their happy place. That's okay. If we hold on to the old ways, we will never embrace the new, and given the importance of our mental fitness, if the future of selling doesn't fit, look for something that does fit.

For those of us excited about the future, Infinite Selling presents a vibrant and engaging opportunity to offer our products and services to people who truly need them, enabling both buyers and sellers to succeed.

There is such freedom in no longer feeling the guilt of selling something we don't want to sell, or using techniques and methods that are nothing short of manipulation. It's a new world, and we are the pioneers that can change the face of this profession and leave behind what was.

Outside of the sales process and methodologies, the other fundamental change we need to embrace is the concept of revenue, not sales.
This is such an important concept to embrace as it frees us from the old
silos and destructive competition between sales and marketing.

The more we realize that the goal is to generate and realize revenue, the more we can work together, collaborate, share goals, and share
success.

I know I've mentioned it before, but I still find it astonishing the
level of self-interest that is generated when we pitch sales and marketing departments against each other, with each side blaming the other
side for the poor performance by evidencing they've done their part.
Its self-defeating.

If one fails, we all fail. Without revenue, we have nothing.

It's better for us to stop pushing the roundabout and be brave
enough to acknowledge that the two chiefdoms need each other in a
wonderful symbiotic relationship that, rather than bringing conflict,
brings an organization together under a common goal to get the right
product, to the right person, at the right time.

And, of course, when we do that, we all succeed.

And that's why we chose the Infinite Loop to describe how we see
revenue generation and realization. It's a constant movement between
two areas, flowing with ease and flow. To use a little bit of poetic licence,
it's like a dance – a fluid motion between positions, between buyer and
seller, between revenue generation and revenue realization.

I appreciate that I may have lost a few of you in that last statement,
but done right, there is something so wonderful and powerful in how
this can be executed.

The key to all of this is not just on the seller. In fact, I would say that
is the smaller part of the picture. The greatest responsibility has to fall
on management and leadership. Without support at the highest level,
while success will still be possible, it will not thrive.

This is because unless the entire revenue organization embraces
this new world, its effectiveness is reduced significantly. I'll make no

bones about it; this is transformation and will require much bravery to implement.

There is heavy lifting to be done across the organization, but it starts at the top. It starts with leadership understanding the need to embed mental fitness as a foundation, and to embrace the concept of revenue instead of the traditional sales and marketing silos.

From the senior leadership, it then needs to roll down to the individual departmental leaders. And this is where we have always seen the most resistance. Here, the leaders have earned their stripes in the old ways and are usually very reluctant to move from what they have known to be successful. And who can blame them? Not many have the stones to move from what they know works to enter the unknown, particularly if it will involve effort.

And this will require effort, but as discussed in right at the beginning, the benefits are clear.

At this level, though, it is really where the rubber hits the road. If leaders fully and genuinely embrace the positions outlined in this book, they can make or break it.

Over the last two decades, Matt and I have had the privilege to watch many hundreds of enablement programmes and transformations being put in place, and the lynchpin for success is always right here, with the leaders. However, we know from bitter experience that if this layer of leadership has a half-baked commitment to the cause, the transformation will fall.

But we also know that those who embrace the change in their hearts and cores are by far the most successful. We are asking a lot here, however. We are ripping up old rules and guardrails that protected us and provided for our families, and all for the reward of hard work. What could possibly go wrong?!

One of the ways we can solve this problem is to ensure we are engaged from the onset at all levels. This isn't a new concept; we have been doing this for years by trying to encourage leaders to be mentors.

As we close, firstly, I want to thank you for getting all the way to the end. But mostly, I want to thank you for taking the journey with us. Over the years, selling is an essential and noble profession that has gathered a reputation that doesn't reflect its value in society.

If we are brave enough to apply the principles in this book, there is a chance we can build a new sense of pride in being a seller, but we can only do that when we stop thinking about selling as sales but rather focus on the value we bring to the buyer and to the larger social and economic environments.

We should be able to be proud to say we are in the business of selling, and proud to be associated with the art and skill that we know is involved.

Moreover, our businesses will benefit – from larger sales, quicker sales, and more frequent sales.

Infinite Selling is not just a methodology or business process; it's an ethos. And like any ethos, it will require effort and energy and will challenge you to the core, but our promise to you is that if you see it through, the world of revenue realization will change. It will open up a whole new reality.

Go on, I dare you.

Works cited

Aberdeen Strategy & Research (2016). *I Achieved the Holy Grail of Sales and Marketing Alignment... or So I Thought*. Retrieved from www.aberdeen.com/cmo-essentials/i-achieved-the-holy-grail-of-sales-and-marketing-alignmentor-so-i-thought/

AlDosiry, K. S., Alkhadher, O. H., AlAqraa', E. M. and Anderson, N. (2016). Relationships between emotional intelligence and sales performance in Kuwait. *Journal of Business and Psychology*, 32(1): 39–45. Retrieved from www.elsevier.es/en-revista-revista-psicologia-del-trabajo-organizaciones-370-articulo-relationships-between-emotio nal-intelligence-sales-S1576596215000638#:~:text=The%20EI%20 and%20sales%20revenue,a%20result%20of%20market%20influences

Centre for Mental Health. (2024). *The Economic and Social Costs of Mental Ill Health*. Retrieved from www.centreformentalhealth.org.uk/ publications/the-economic-and-social-costs-of-mental-ill-health/

Chamine, S. (2012). *Positive Intelligence: Why Only 20% of Teams and Individuals Achieve Their True Potential and How You Can Achieve Yours*. Greenleaf Book Press.

Clear, J. (2018). *Atomic Habits*. Random House Business.

Covey, S. R. (2004). *The 7 Habits of Highly Effective People*. Simon & Schuster.

CRM, D. (2016). *Need a More Predictable Pipeline? Only Hard Data Will Do It*. Retrieved from www.destinationcrm.com/Articles/Web-Exclusives/Viewpoints/Need-a-More-Predictable-Pipeline-Only-Hard-Data-Will-Do-It-110630.aspx

Deloitte. (2023). *Understanding Generation Z in the Workplace.* Retrieved from www.deloitte.com/us/en/Industries/consumer/articles/understanding-generation-z-in-the-workplace.html

Deloitte. (2024). *The Projected Costs and Economic Impact of Mental Health Inequities in the United States.* Retrieved from www.deloitte.com/us/en/insights/industry/health-care/economic-burden-mental-health-inequities.html

Dweck, C. S. (2006). *Mindset: The New Psychology of Success.* Random House.

Emmons, R. A. (2003). Counting blessings versus burdens: An experimental investigation of gratitude and subjective well-being in daily life. *Journal of Personality and Social Psychology*, 84(2): 377–389.

Forbes. (2014). *The Role of Influence in the New Buyer's Journey.* Retrieved from www.forbes.com/sites/danielnewman/2014/04/10/the-role-of-influence-in-the-new-buyers-journey/

Forbes. (2015). *Competition at Work: Positive or Positively Awful?* Retrieved from www.forbes.com/sites/work-in-progress/2015/07/08/competition-at-work-positive-or-positively-awful/

Forrester. (2024). *Forrester's B2B Marketing & Sales Predictions 2025.* Retrieved from www.forrester.com/press-newsroom/forrester-predictions-2025-b2b-marketing-sales/

Gallup. (2017). *State of the American Manager.* Retrieved from www.gallup.com/services/182138/state-american-manager.aspx

Gartner. (2021). *A Step Beyond the Challenger Sale.* Retrieved from www.gartner.com/en/sales-service/insights/challenger-sale

Gartner. (2022). *Gartner Identifies 7 Technology Disruptions That Will Impact Sales Through 2027*. Retrieved from www.gartner.com/en/newsroom/press-releases/2022-10-10-gartner-identifies-seven-technology-disruptions-that-will-impact-sales-through-2027#:~:text=By%202025%2C%2080%25%20of%20B2B,product%20demonstrations%20and%20sales%20training

Gartner. (2024). *Key Trends Driving Customer Experience in 2025*. Retrieved from www.gartner.com/en/documents/5842447

Gartner. (2025a). *Chief Sales Officers Must Adapt as B2B Buyers Choose Digital Self-Service Over Seller*. Retrieved from www.gartner.com/en/newsroom/press-releases/2025-06-25-gartner-sales-survey-finds-61-percent-of-b2b-buyers-prefer-a-rep-free-buying-experience

Gartner. (2025b). *Companies are Using AI to Make Faster Decisions in Sales and Marketing*. Retrieved from https://hbr.org/2025/06/companies-are-using-ai-to-make-faster-decisions-in-sales-and-marketing

Gartner. (n.d.). *Revenue Intelligence (Transitioning to Revenue Action Orchestration)*. Retrieved from www.gartner.com/reviews/market/revenue-intelligence

Goleman, D. (1995). *Emotional Intelligence: Why It Can Matter More Than IQ*. Bloomsbury.

Harvard. (2024). *How to Build – and Improve – Company Culture*. Retrieved from https://professional.dce.harvard.edu/blog/how-to-build-and-improve-company-culture/

Harvard Business Review. (2015). *The New Science of Customer Emotions*. Retrieved from https://hbr.org/2015/11/the-new-science-of-customer-emotions

Journal of Business and Industrial Marketing. (2020). *Effect of Internal Competitive Work Environment on Working Smart and Emotional Exhaustion: The Moderating Role of Time Management.* Retrieved from www.researchgate.net/publication/346805560_Effect_of_internal_competitive_work_environment_on_working_smart_and_emotional_exhaustion_the_moderating_role_of_time_management

Journal of Marketing Research. (2022). *Fostering Creative Selling Through Ethics. An Emotion-based Approach.* Retrieved from https://onlinelibrary.wiley.com/doi/10.1111/beer.12491.

Journal of Psychology. (2013). *The Effects of Individual and Team Competitions on Performance, Emotions, and Effort.* Retrieved from www.researchgate.net/publication/236087428_The_Effects_of_Individual_and_Team_Competitions_on_Performance_Emotions_and_Effort#:~:text=Results%20indicated%20that%20performance%2C%20enjoyment,by%20increased%20enjoyment%20and%20effort

Marketo. (2021). *Marketo Success Series: Lead Scoring.* Retrieved from https://nation.marketo.com/t5/product-blogs/marketo-success-series-lead-scoring/ba-p/309849

McKinsey & Company. (2021). *Pricing and Promotions: The Analytics Opportunity.* Retrieved from www.mckinsey.com/capabilities/growth-marketing-and-sales/our-insights/pricing-and-promotions-the-analytics-opportunity

McKinsey & Company. (2025). *Unlocking Profitable B2B Growth Through Gen AI.* Retrieved from www.mckinsey.com/capabilities/growth-marketing-and-sales/our-insights/unlocking-profitable-b2b-growth-through-gen-ai

McKinsey Health Institute. (2025). *Investing in the Future: How Better Mental Health Benefits Everyone.* Retrieved from www.mckinsey.com/mhi/our-insights/investing-in-the-future-how-better-mental-health-benefits-everyone

Mullainathan, S. (2013). *Scarcity: Why Having Too Little Means So Much*. Times Books.

Norris, C. J., Creem, D., Hendler, R., Kober, H. (2018). Brief mindfulness meditation improves attention in novices: Evidence from ERPs and moderation by neuroticism. *Frontiers in Human Neuroscience*. doi: 10.3389/fnhum.2018.00315

RoSPA. (2024). *The Hidden Costs of Presenteeism*. Retrieved from www.truworthwellness.com/blog/hidden-costs-of-presenteeism/

Seligman, M. E. (2018). *Learned Optimism: How to Change Your Mind and Your Life*. Vintage.

Today, P. (2024). *The Psychology of Competitiveness*. Retrieved from www.psychologytoday.com/gb/blog/here-there-and-everywhere/202408/the-psychology-of-competitiveness

World Health Organization. (2024). *Mental Health at Work*. Retrieved from www.who.int/news-room/fact-sheets/detail/mental-health-at-work

Acknowledgements

Matt and I would like to acknowledge and personally thank everyone at Mentor Group who has helped us and inspired and supported us in writing this book, including Jane Hall, Jack Smith, Jim McManus, Chris Norton, Neil Kelly, Steve Promisel, Alison Loring, Ben Barton, Ben Wild, David Cuffley, Duncan McNeil, Hannah Rolls, Harriet Guojah, Kirsty McEwan, Lewis Jones, Lorna Quelch, Mark Burge, Rebecca Bromley, Richard Keown, Shanice Blower, Shirley Densham, Simon Jackson, Sophie Dyer, Zoë Bryson, Zoe Munt, Charlie Robinson, Kathryn Hoverd, Matthew Cheung, Nadia Akhtar, Amy Patel, Harvey Laird, and Surjit Kooner.

We would also like to acknowledge those who have stood by us and inspired us over the years, including Tim Shaw, Jim and Lari Davidson, Mike Burt, and Kris Coppock.

And, of course, all those close to us for putting up with us and our commitment to this project.

Special thanks to Emily Barton for the illustrations you will have found throughout this book.

About the authors

James A. Barton

James began his career in HR right after college and quickly transformed the HR department by introducing technology to automate processes and procedures. This path led him to a career in technology, and after a few consultancy roles, he advanced to the position of Director of IT and E-Business for a Premiership football club.

He was then offered a role to start a new company and serve as their Sales Director, marking the beginning of his career in sales. After six years, this led him to Mentor Group, where he joined as a consultant specializing in developing innovative solutions that integrated technology with sales enablement.

James is now the Chief Solutions Officer at Mentor Group and continues to innovate and build solutions to help sellers improve their skills for Mentor's clients worldwide.

Matt Webb

Matt has been on the front lines of sales since he began his career in 1994, working for Vodafone. After 12 years, he gradually rose to the position of sales manager, overseeing both business and corporate sales channels.

In 2007, Matt joined Mentor Group, which specializes in sales, leadership, and management transformation. During that time, he held various positions, including account management for key clients, programme design, and working as a delivery specialist.

Matt is now the CEO of Mentor Group, and his superpower is collaborating with the C Suite to drive significant revenue transformation.

Index

A quick word from Practical Inspiration Publishing...

We hope you found this book both practical and inspiring – that's what we aim for with every book we publish.

We publish titles on topics ranging from leadership, entrepreneurship, HR and marketing to self-development and wellbeing.

Find details of all our books at: www.practicalinspiration.com

Did you know...

We can offer discounts on bulk sales of all our titles – ideal if you want to use them for training purposes, corporate giveaways or simply because you feel these ideas deserve to be shared with your network.

We can even produce bespoke versions of our books, for example with your organization's logo and/or a tailored foreword.

To discuss further, contact us on info@practicalinspiration.com.

Got an idea for a business book?

We may be able to help. Find out about more about publishing in partnership with us at: bit.ly/PIpublishing.

Follow us on social media…

@PIPTalking

@pip_talking

@practicalinspiration

@piptalking

Practical Inspiration Publishing

www.ingramcontent.com/pod-product-compliance
Lightning Source LLC
Chambersburg PA
CBHW021921190326
41519CB00009B/868